LOSTMANS
HERITAGE

PIONEERS in the FLORIDA EVERGLADES

Revised Edition

Karen Yvonne Hamilton

Yesterday Press

Acclaim for Lostmans Heritage:

Janet Naughten, professor of history – *Hamilton's years of research, interviews, primary documents, local lore and carefully constructed hypothesis makes this a solid and entertaining book. I was immediately transported into the mysterious Everglades wilderness and immersed in the details of Hamilton's colorful ancestors. This compelling Florida pioneer story reads like a novel, yet it is all true, based on newspaper accounts, government records, depositions and interviews. Hamilton's work is a much needed and welcome addition to South Florida's 19th and early 20th century history.*

Tyrrell L. Armstrong, author and historian - *First class genealogical record of an incredible family tree. From the hazy depths of one of Florida's most mysterious and celebrated venues comes this story of the dis-enfranchised, who carved out a living and a hard-nosed way of life in the wilderness of the Everglades. The author is a descendant of the hard-scrabble Hamilton clan, whose existence almost made them non-persons because of their ethnicity. Hamilton does a stellar job recounting the stories of her ancestors over generations with candor and first-person recollections.*

Other titles by Karen Yvonne Hamilton

36 Days: A Memoir

Lifetales: A Workbook for Writing Lifestories

The Barrett Files: A Civil War Pension Case

Cooking with the Ancestors: Recipes & Kitchen Advice from 19th Century Florida

The terrain is silent, the characters are silent,
the past a quiet echo forever being erased by secrets.
We have no answers, yet seek the answers,
and we encounter only what remains. There is nothing left
but the ghosts who refuse to speak.

--Karen Yvonne Hamilton

Dedicated to my ancestors, pioneers of the Florida Everglades, and to my father, Ernest Eugene Hamilton, who grew up in the Ten Thousand Islands in the decade before the Everglades became a national park and taught me to never give up.

Acknowledgements

This book would never have been completed without the invaluable assistance of my sister, Mona Hamilton McMahon and my father, Ernest Hamilton. I don't know how I would have untangled all of these stories without them. My father kept me writing and writing, my sister traveled all over with me, tracing the ancestors from Springfield, Georgia to Key West.

My family was right behind me throughout the journey, and I thank them all for putting up with me and offering encouragement along the way: Hal Simmons, Josephine Garcia Simmons, Nancy Bell Hamilton, Paul Gomes, Ernie Hamilton, Gary Rager, and all my 'cousins' in the Facebook 'Florida Everglades History' group.

A huge 'thank you' for sharing their vast historical knowledge with me and encouraging me as I researched and wrote go to Thomas Locklear, director of Collier County Museum in Everglades City; Tom Hambright, archivist at Key West Library; Capt. Carl "Fizz" Fismer, writer and treasure diver; John Redman, graphic designer; all of the people in libraries, museums, and historical events who cheered me on; and extra special thank yous to my numerous treasure hunter friends across the country.

And finally, thank you to my biggest fans who listened to me drone on incessantly about 'the book': my sons, Joseph Rager, Joshua Rager, Jesse Rager, and my friends, Sharon Moody, Deborah Shultz, and Thomas Gidus.

Family Charts

These family charts are always a work in progress. Much of the information here has been verified through birth, death, government records, etc., but not all of it. Some of it comes from family charts I obtained from other family members, and I have not verified the accuracy of yet. As everything that you read in this book, I give you what I have.

That being said, if anyone reading this finds errors in the genealogy, please email me at kyvonnehamilton@gmail.com so that I may update my files and share with others.

Edwards

William Pitts Edwards 1811-1887 --- Eleanor Southwell 1812-1861

When William Pitts Edwards was born on February 20, 1811, in Effingham, Georgia, his father, Obadiah, was 33 and his mother, Tabitha Pitts, was 28. He married Eleanor Southwell and they had ten children together. He also had one son with Peggy Hamilton. He also had one daughter with Harriet Haseltine Mixson. He died on November 21, 1887, in Alachua, Florida, having lived a long life of 76 years, and was buried in Alachua, Florida.

Ann Haseltine b. 1832
Elvira Amanda Lee b. 1834

Adoniram Judson b. 1836
Frances Julia b. 1838
John Southwell b. 1839
Eliza Burton b. 1841
Laura K b. 1843
Henrietta b. 1845
George William b. 1848
Joseph Newton b. 1851

William Pitts Edwards --- Peggy Hamilton (slave)

Richard Edward Hamilton

Gomes

Francisco Gomes (1855-1931) --- Laura Etta Young (1875-1955)

Francisco Gomes D'sa was born on April 24, 1855, in Bacelos, Braga, Portugal, the son of Mary and H. He married Laura Etta Young on January 14, 1889, in Fort Myers, Florida. They had 12 children in 25 years. He died on June 20, 1931, in Fort Myers, Florida, at the age of 76, and was buried there.

When Laura Etta Young was born on January 22, 1875, in Pensacola, Florida, her father, William, was 23, and her mother, Marie, was 26. She was married several times. She died on September 23, 1955, in Fort Myers, Florida, at the age of 80, and was buried there. Other spouses were Joseph F. Pacetti, Vivian F. McKinney, and Louis J. Reel.

Anna Bell 1890-1965
Mary Joaquina 1895-1971
Joaquin 'King' 1898-1975
Lillian Josephine 1899-1978
Salvador Sabino 1903-1966
Amelia 'Mellie' Isabelle 1907-1975
Florinda Marie 1909-1964
Frances Lenora 1912-1979
Edna 1915-1936

Joaquin 'King' Gomes (1898-1975) --- Nellie Hamilton (1905-1978)

William Leo 'Son' 1923-
Vernon P. 1926-1973
Harold Ray 1934-1991
Franklin D. R. 1939-
Nellie Paula 1947-
Joaquin F. Jr.

Salvador Gomes (1903-1966) --- Rosalie M. Hamilton (1911-1965)

Virginia 1927
Frank 1931
Paul 1937

Hamilton

Eugene Joseph Hamilton (1883-1966) --- Rebecca Johnson (1887-1947)

When Rebecca Elizabeth Johnson was born on March 27, 1887, in Clearwater, Florida, her father, Gilbert, was 29, and her mother, Mellisa, was 25. She married Eugene Joseph Hamilton on February 8, 1903, in Lee, Florida. They had nine children in 19 years. She died on April 11, 1947, in Everglades City, Florida, at the age of 60, and was buried in Fort Myers Florida.

William Joseph 1904-1932
Nellie M. 1905-1978
Ellen Cathleen 1908-1963
Rosalie M. 1911-1965
Eugene Joseph 1913-1991
Ethel Madelyn 1914-1964
Irene Elizabeth 1917-1993
Roy Philip 1921-1969
Eugene Mervin 1923-2013

John Leon Hamilton (1885-1964) --- Sarah Elizabeth Johnson (1889-1963)

Mary 1907-unknown
Eva Margaret 1909-1979
Robert Joseph 1913- 1932
Adeline Agnes 1915-1949
Henry Gilbert 1915-1989
Elizabeth Ann 'Lizzie' 1918-1970
Raymond 1930-
Bryan 1932-

Richard Hamilton (1840-1944) --- Hannah Elizabeth Moore (1845-1920)

William E. 1870-unknown
George Lewis 1872-1950
Thomas C. 1873-1951
Jane 'Julia' 1874-unknown
Benjamin L. 1876-unknown
Walter Joseph Valentine 1880-1957
Robert 1883-unknown
Nina 1885-unknown

Richard Hamilton (1840-1944) --- Mary Appolonia Weeks (1859-1917)

When Mary Appolonia Weeks was born in July 1859 in Everglades City, Florida, her father, John, was 26, and her mother, Sarah, was 17. She married George L. Christian and they had two children together. She then married Richard Edward Hamilton and they had six children together. She died on September 13, 1917, in Florida at the age of 58, and was buried in Collier, Florida.

Walter Joseph Valentine 1880-1957
Eugene Joseph Hamilton 1883-1966
John Leon Hamilton 1885-1964
Mary Elizabeth 1888-1968
Ann Elizabeth 1893-1970
Mary Agnes 1895-1953

Walter Joseph Valentine Hamilton --- Minnie Hamilton (1884-unknown)

Marie Violet 1913-1980
Annie Thelma 1917-1964
Edna 1919-unknown

Walter Joseph Valentine Hamilton --- Lettie Pent (1880-1922)

Edna Cecelia 1919-1969

William Joseph Hamilton (1904-1932) --- Florinda Marie Gomes (1909-1964)

When Florinda Marie Gomes was born on November 2, 1909, in Boca Grande, Florida, her father, Francisco, was 54, and her mother, Laura Young, was 34. She married William Hamilton on January 27, 1927 in Fort Myers, Florida. After Williams death in 1932, she married William David Parker in 1933 in Charlotte, Florida. They divorced in 1942. She then married Junius Otto Posey and they had two children, Junius and Thomas, together. She died on July 26, 1964, in Palm Beach, Florida, at the age of 54, and was buried in Key West, Florida.

William Joseph, Jr. 1926-1992
Francis Salvador Theodore 1929-1978
Ernest Eugene b. 1932-

Johnson

Gilbert Henry Johnson (1857-1934)--- Mellisa Emaline Holland (1862-1930)

Gilbert Henry Johnson was born on July 13, 1857, in Harbour Island, Bahamas. He married Mellisa Emaline Holland on August 19, 1886, in Tampa, Florida. He died on August 25, 1934, in Miami, Florida, at the age of 77.

When Mellisa Emaline Holland was born in 1862 in McRae, Georgia, her father, Henry, was 37, and her mother, Elizabeth Hodge, was 23. She died in 1930 in Florida at the age of 68.

Rebecca Elizabeth 1887-1947
Sarah Elizabeth 1889-1963
Gilbert Jr. 1891-unknown
Joseph Christopher 1897-1972

Weeks[1]

John Leon Weeks (1832-1900) --- Deborah Tanner (1818-unknown)

John Leon Weeks --- Sarah Ann Mercer Raulerson (1843-1865)

James 1858-unknown
Mary Appolonia 1859-1917
Henry 1860-unknown

---

[1] This data is still in active research mode.

Stephen W. 1862-unknown
John W. 1864- J
P. M. 1865-unknown
Mary 1868-unknown
Isaac 1873-unknown
Annie 1878-unknown
Benjamin 1881-unknown

John Weeks --- Mary Elizabeth 'Lizzie' Raulerson[2]

Matthew Weeks b. 1881
David Weeks b. 1883
Josephine b. 1885
William b. 1887
Alfred b. 1889
John b. 1893
Mary Elizabeth b. 1895

[2] This data is taken directly from Faye Brown's book, *Weeks Family Connections.*

Contents

Foreword

BEGINNINGS

Researching a family history is a maze of surprises around every corner. At best we are able to find facts and statistics that recreate a general foundation to build on. I find the older the source, even news articles, the more trustworthy the information is. I won't say that I trust every news article that I read, but these at least give me something to start with other than family lore. Tales passed down through the generations tend to be biased, exaggerated, or both, like the classic game of 'telephone.'

Still, in the end, all that we can do is imagine the rest, fill in the missing pieces with generalities that might have occurred. English historian G. Kitson Clark once said that these generalizations are "necessarily founded on guesses, guesses informed by much general reading and relevant knowledge, guesses shaped by much brooding on the matter in hand, but on guesses nonetheless."[1] As I venture into the tangled maze that constitutes my ancestry, this is how I feel. Everything here comes from many years of research and countless debates with others following this story. As Peter Matthiessen said in an interview once, "There is nothing here that *couldn't* have

---

[1] Novick, Peter. 1988. *That Noble Dream.*

happened."[2] Based on the facts. Based on family lore. Based on historical documents. I promise I will keep as close to the edge of truth as I possibly can. And when I tip over the edge a tiny bit, I'll let you know I'm doing so.

Here you will find stories though, as many of the stories that I could find. In addition to facts garnered from the usual government documents, I have tried to gather 'stories' from across families, families who have never met before. Therefore, when four different people from separate families tell me the same 'family' story, I feel I get closer to truth, get closer to offering you the truth the best we can hope to know it from this distance of time.

I'm often asked, "Why are you writing this book?" Valid question. It is one that I answer with some difficulty, however. I have many reasons for wanting to see this book out in the world, so I find it frustrating to pin down just one exact reason for all the years of research, writing, and rewriting. If you are going to insist that I give you one, I would have to say because the ghosts won't stop nudging me.

My father, Ernest Eugene Hamilton, always says, "Make your mark." He certainly has done that. Born in the poorest section of Key West, he spent his childhood shuffled among relatives ranging from Key West to Lostmans to Fort Myers. His father, William Joseph Hamilton (Buddy), would have been one of the last of the residents of the Ten Thousand Islands before the National Park Service took over. I say "would have" because Papa disappeared in the dark swamp at Shark Point in 1932, his body never found. My father was born seven months later. My grandmother, Florinda, tried to stay there in the Glades, near Lostmans River, and raise her three boys, but it was very hard for a woman alone with three small boys in those swamps.

---

[2] Watson, James G. "Man Writing: The Watson Trilogy: Peter Matthiessen in Archive." Page 247

My father rose above the loss of his father, the displaced childhood, the poverty. He joined the service, graduated from University of Florida with an accounting degree, married and raised children, became 'someone' in his community. He made his mark.

My ancestors who arrived in the Florida Everglades shortly after the Civil War and built a "tribe" did something amazing in the decades they homesteaded in the islands. They thrived in an environment that was dangerous and wild and ever changing. While others came and went, the Hamilton family faced every challenge nature and man threw at them and carried on. They may have migrated from island to island now and again, but the Everglades were their home.

You'll find them mentioned here and there in the many books written about the Glades. In a 1959 article, historian Charlton Tebeau, says, "The Hamiltons, to the disappointment of the romanticists, were neither pirates nor smugglers nor fugitives, but simple fishermen. They worked the abundant schools off the coast until 1947, when they were forced to evacuate their homesites by the establishment of the Everglades National Park."[3] There were two Hamilton families in the Everglades, but Tebeau was talking about the Richard Hamilton family, my ancestors. Tebeau was fascinated by my family, and he referred to them many times as one of the 'lost tribes' of the islands.

But it wasn't until Peter Matthiessen wrote *Killing Mr. Watson* that the Hamilton tribe leapt into the public eye. And now when I say, "I am a descendent of Richard Hamilton," eyes light up and people say, "Oh! You're one of Matthiessen's Hamiltons!"

---

[3] Ash, Clarke. "U-M Prof Traces White Settlers In Remote Corners of Everglades." Page 10

And this is what haunts me. They were more than the fictionalized version of them. I want to tell what I know about these men and women who are my family. I want to take what Matthiessen started and tell you what I know about my ancestors, where they came from, what the world was like around them, and what the stories are that they passed down through the generations.

This is their mark, and I want to leave it for them. They were extraordinary. They were brave. They were dangerous. They were pioneers.

That is what I call my noble mission. But it is not why I started researching my family or writing this book. I approached genealogy with a single purpose in mind. To discover where my surname, Hamilton, originated. I had visions of tracing my name to some foreign country, to some long dead ancestor who earned the name in the olden days. I began with my father's side of the family because I had been raised with tales of life in the Everglades during the Great Depression. I couldn't imagine why my ancestors would have chosen such a wilderness to make their home. I only made it back six generations.

As I uncovered each paternal ancestor, I grew more and more excited. What fascinating characters! Like actors on the stage, I could picture them in my mind. I was held at rapt attention as they performed their lives for me through family stories, census records, and engravings on tombstones. But as I approached the fifth generation, my great-great grandfather, my awe turned to shock. I read in Mr. Tebeau's book, *Man in the Everglades*, that Richard had served in the Union army, so I decided to order his military records from the National Archives. A few weeks later, I opened the mailbox to find a large, thick brown envelope. The name on every page was *not* Richard Hamilton. It was Stephen Barrett. I recall being annoyed; they had sent me the *wrong* records. Several phone calls later, I finally reached someone who asked me, "Have you read through all the documents?"

Well, I had not. I was brand new to doing genealogy. So, I settled down and began reading. There are times when researching one's family history that you find surprises, fascinating characters who defy all logic and confound and astonish the researcher. Richard Hamilton is one such character. The most astonishing characteristic of Richard that I stumbled on was that he was a slave. He was also a fugitive from justice, having filed for a Civil War pension under someone else's name. In my wildest dreams, I had not imagined that I was directly descended from slavery. Of all the research scenarios, tracing the genealogy of slaves was tantamount to impossible! Or was it? While I didn't expect to encounter a slave nestled amongst my family tree, there was Richard, hiding just out of reach, leaving behind him mystery and suppositions regarding his life. He had quite a few aliases as well - Robert Hamilton, R.E. Hamilton, Richard Hambelton, and Stephen Barrett to name the most used ones.

I dug in my heels and found myself awash in the life of a fascinating man, an extraordinary and dangerous man, a man who, against all odds, untangled himself from the bonds of slavery and began a family and a life in the Florida Everglades. The Everglades itself is shrouded in mysteries, a tangle of mangroves, waterways, and sawgrass that meanders every which way and is as mutable as the wind. Nothing is ever where you left it. This was where one came to get lost, to hide amongst the wild things and the Seminoles. Here, in this place, was where I found my ancestors. Not much remains of them there. A few artifacts like old engine parts and coquina blocks they used for cisterns. And stories. So many stories. Bootlegging, murders, gangsters, killers, and tales of tomahawks and missing schoolteachers.

Beginnings

Out on one of the Keys there is a large, profusely blooming Royal Poinciana tree. I was thrilled to find an old video taken in 1995 that shows that tree. Family lore says that under that tree is where Richard Hamilton is buried, along with his wife, Mary, a child, and a man from another Key. Some say the tree is still there, but it is dead now, some 90 years later. Others say that Hurricane Irma carried it off for good. The little graveyard is so overgrown that it is near impossible to wander through it, if you can even find it. Hurricanes and government interventions tend to relocate even land in the Ten Thousand Islands. Many in our family, including me, know the exact place, the exact Key where the cemetery lies, but we're going to keep that secret.

I think about these people and the ones who laid these souls to rest under the perpetual shade of the Poinciana, and I want to tell their stories, let their ghosts speak. I feel a sense of duty, familial pride that never lets me forget where I came from. I still have a long way to go - but that is the joy of genealogy - the work is never complete. With a little ingenuity, there is always more to uncover, more fascinating roots to dig up.

Chapter 1

BLOODLINES

If you have to start somewhere, the beginning is as good a place as any. To tell Richard's story, or in his case, stories, it is necessary for us to transport back to the mid-1800s. Here is where my great-great grandfather, Richard E. Hamilton,[1] first comes to us, a child born into slavery in Effingham County, Georgia. Not one of the best places to end up if you were a slave. Georgia in the 1840s, where Richard spent his early years of life, was not a place one wanted to be if you were anything other than white. And preferably well off. Georgia at this time had one of the highest percentages of slaves in the United States, second only to Virginia. In 1840, the slave population was 280,944 and doubled in size by the start of the Civil War. The production of cotton and rice was the bedrock of Georgia's economy, and the producers of those items largely found ways to get around the 1808 edict banning slave importation.[2]

Born in the 1840s near Savannah, Georgia, Richard spent his first years on a series of farms owned by William Pitts Edwards. I decided to push back a bit farther in my research than William Edwards because I wanted a better sense of the

---

[1] Different documents list Richard's middle name alternately as Eugene or Edward.
[2] Young, Jeffrey R. "Slavery in Antebellum Georgia."

family that Richard came from and perhaps find a clue as to why the Edwards family left Georgia in 1850.

Fig. 1.1 William Pitts Edwards

Land records show the locations of Edwards' father, Obadiah Edwards' properties in Springfield, GA, roughly 20 miles NW of Savannah. As of 1826, Obadiah owned 700 acres of pine land which put him in the planter class. Generally, owning at least 200 to 500 acres put one in this class. In 1830 and 1840, Obadiah didn't have any slaves and his primary business was agriculture.[3] I was able to find one slave schedule that lists six slaves owned by Obadiah in 1850, three adults and three children.[4] This number kept the Edwards family out of the yeoman class, which consisted of farms with under five slaves and less than 100 acres of land.

Edwards was 29 when Richard was born, he had been married to Eleanor Southwell for nine years, and they owned one female slave. That slave was listed on the census as between 10-24. Peggy, Richard's mother would have been about 21 that year. Based on depositions and interviews of former slaves, we can make an inference that Peggy was a house slave. As records of these details are non-existent, I noted that Peggy was likely a 'half breed,' possibly part Indian, highly possibly black. The children of William Edwards speak

---

[3] Georgia. Effingham County. 1840 U. S. Census. Page: 143
[4] Slave Schedules. 1850 U.S. Federal Census

fondly of her, which means she had more than the usual contact with them than a field hand would have.

Peggy "was a full blood Choctaw Indian," states Richard in 1902. From various documents, we can estimate that she was born in Georgia around 1820. Little else is known of Peggy's early background or how she came to be a slave. Queries to the Native American reservations have been a dead end. With few records of Peggy anywhere, there is no way to find out what her Choctaw name was (or even if she was in fact Choctaw) or how she received the name Peggy Hamilton. On the early slave census', she is always listed as *B* (black).

When 'Cap'n Billy,' as William Edwards was known to the slaves, left Springfield in 1850, there were only 12 houses, a courthouse and a jail in the town. Edwards' land value in Springfield was $900 according to the 1850 Effingham County census. Richard later says, "Edwards owned a number of slaves. I remember one named Sophia and one named Sarah.

He did not have but one or two men, I do not remember them."[5]

Map 1.1 Springfield, Georgia year[6]

It is not clear what years Richard was talking about, probably after moving to Florida.

In June of 1850, William Edwards owned four slaves: one woman aged 30, one girl aged 10, one boy aged 7, and another boy aged 2. So, all we can do here is make an assumption, a

---

[5] *Deposition D*. Richard Hamilton.

[6] Williams. Bonner's map of the State of Georgia with the addition of its geological features. 1849.

guess, that the woman mentioned on the 1850 slave schedule may have been, could have been, Peggy. If Richard was born in the early 1840s, then the 7-year-old boy could be him. The ages are very close. Henrietta Edwards Jones, William Edwards' daughter says, "He (Richard) was born the 26th day of July 1848. We had a record of births, but it was burned some years ago."[7] Judson Edwards, William Edwards' son was born in 1851 and he says, "I do not know Richards exact age, but he was about three years older than I."[8] If we believe the Edwards legitimate children, then Richard was the 2-year-old on that 1850 census, which sets his birth year at 1848, not the early '40s as Richard states later.

Here is where I have to take a breather because my head is spinning. The interesting (maddening) thing about this type of research is that one question may yield the answer you've been looking for, but it also frequently yields several more questions. Who is the other little boy and the little girl? Peggy's children as well? No relation at all? Census records before 1870 were not required to list names of slaves. We don't know the names of the other two children listed on that census. We don't even know if Peggy and Richard's last name was Hamilton. When did Richard acquire that surname? Occasionally, the census taker included the sex and age of slaves, but mostly they were only required to record the number of slaves owned by a resident.

A researcher would have to find the records kept by the slave owner, who usually wrote down the slave's name, age, maybe another fact or two. Unfortunately, fires during the Civil War and subsequent fire incidents over the years destroyed most of those records. I've read many firsthand accounts of slave life from former slaves, and those narratives often offer up information regarding naming, etc.

---

[7] *Deposition K.* Henrietta Edwards Jones.

[8] *Deposition G.* Judson Edwards.

Where did 'Hamilton' come from? When was the first time the name was used? After the Civil War? Possible scenarios: Peggy acquired the name from a former slave owner, Richard's father's name was Hamilton, the name was chosen by Edwards after some other person, Richard (or Peggy) chose the name for themselves. And, was Peggy's surname Edwards or Hamilton before she married and became Peggy Anderson?

Historian Canter Brown writes in one of his books that Richard Hamilton was "possibly…the slave of either George or James Hamilton."[9] This is a logical connection to answer where the surname came from. George and James were brothers who came from Georgia to Florida in the late 1840s. If Richard was a slave of one of the brothers, he would have taken his owner's last name. Brown's short review of Richard Hamilton contains some accurate information about our Richard, but the supposition that Richard spent the majority of his life in Hillsborough County does not match up with the facts that we know of our ancestor. I lean towards believing that there were two Richard Hamilton's and Brown's research possibly jumbled the two together.

Unanswered questions, the sustenance of every genealogist and historian. Some of those questions we must let remain in the shadows. For now.

My sister, Mona and I visited Springfield in 2018. The town lies slightly northwest of Savannah, and the drive out there seemed to roll on forever. We had recently left Williston, Florida, which would be the next stop for Richard. Mona and I were both surprised how similar Springfield and Williston were. The town was small, and we drove around for a while looking for the courthouse. It was closed unfortunately, but I noticed a sign that read "Springfield Historical Museum." A quick left turn from the courthouse and we found a small

---

[9] Brown, pps. 103-105

building resting in front of a chain link fence. Behind the fence was living history.

Beyond the fence were twelve buildings that date from 1790 to 1950. Today the buildings are furnished with artifacts and materials saved from original buildings. Although we did not get a chance to visit them, there is a barn, a blacksmith shop, a carpenter shop, and several houses. We took photos as best we could from our side of the fence, but the museum and all the buildings beyond the fence were closed.

Fig. 1.2 Effingham Living History Museum, Springfield Georgia\i

Fig. 1.3 Effingham Living History Museum Main Building, Springfield Georgia

As we sat in the motorhome deciding what to do next, a young man pulled up in a truck. He opened the gate and went inside. Hoping that we might talk him into letting us in, we got out and approached him as he returned to his truck. We told him who we were and what we were researching.

"You're related to the Edwards?" he asked excitedly. Without going into detail, we admitted that we were. He promptly pulled out his phone, punched in some numbers, and the next thing we knew he was handing the phone over to Mona. "It's my grandfather," he says, "He knows everything about the family."

While we were excited, we quickly realized that the information this 'relative' was telling us was information that we already had. After hanging up, the young man says, "There are a lot of descendants from the Edwards family still living around here. We have an Edwards family reunion every summer."

My heart jumped at that. How exciting to go to a reunion of Edwards descendants! But wait. How do we introduce ourselves? These are the descendants of the man who *owned* our great-great grandfather and great-great-great grandmother! What will they think of us being there? We thanked the young man and agreed to come back another time and maybe even come to the reunion. While we know that records of the Edwards slaves were lost in a fire, we still hold out hope of finding a link that will tell us more about Richard's mother, Peggy Hamilton. Perhaps one of the Edwards' descendants has heard a story or two of her that will tell us more.

It is interesting to note that I began this genealogical research in the early 1980s because I wanted to track the origin of the Hamilton name, and now I will probably never know. Obviously, if Peggy was really a Choctaw Indian, then someone 'gave' her the name of Hamilton. While many dispute that Native Americans were ever held as slaves, countless memoirs and historical documents prove otherwise. Again, Peggy is listed as black on early census records. In the white south of those days, it didn't matter so much whether you were black or Indian; it was enough that you were simply 'other.'

Fig. 1.6 The only known image of Peggy Hamilton

Full blooded Indians were listed on separate census'. The earliest official record we can find of Peggy is the Marion County Florida 1870 census. Her last name is Anderson, she is married, and she has five children. All are listed as 'black' there. There was a distinction made by census takers between *B* for 'black' and *Mu* for 'mulatto.' Each census over the next 30 years lists her as *B*. Never is she listed anywhere on government documents as Indian. On one census record, her birthplace says "Indiana." Could this have been a mistake on the census takers part? When asked the birthplace of his mother, someone may have said, "Indian," and the census taker wrote it down as "Indiana."

As far as we know, Peggy never left the north Florida area. She married Lou (London) Anderson, a black man, in 1848, shortly before arriving in Florida. Their daughter, Lizzie, was born this same year. After arriving in Florida in 1850, four more children were born: Georgianna, Alexander, George, and Andrew. With the exception of Peggy and Lizzie, Lou and all the children are listed as farmhands on the 1870 Ocala census. Lou died in 1870. Peggy's last known address was Elmwood, FL and she is supposedly buried on the Edwards estate in Williston, Florida.

On Richard's baptismal certificate, dated 1877, Peggy is listed as Chickasaw and his father is listed as Wm. Edwards.

But Richard was an adult convert to the Catholic faith and filled out the baptismal certificate himself, so we can't exactly take his word for anything at this point.

Whether or not William Pitts Edwards is part of the Hamilton lineage is debatable. G. H. Watson (not to be confused with the infamous Edgar J. Watson) of Everglades, Florida says of Richard in a letter dated 1902 that "his (Richard's) history can be traced back to when he was a slave. His father being his owner, whose name was Edwards." Richard claims that Edwards was his biological father, but Edwards' legitimate heirs claim otherwise.

Edwards' son, Judson, recalls, "His (Richard) father was a light mulatto and belonged to Mr. Frederick (the last name is unreadable) of Effingham Co."[10]

Richard describes Edwards as "a dark-skinned man" with "very dark curly hair." Richard himself has stated that his father was half Portuguese and owned several slaves. Another time, in the encounter with Ed Watson, he says his father was half Creek Indian.

Following the Edwards lineage back, I find no evidence that the family was ever in Portugal at all. They certainly were not of Native American blood. Records on Edwards do not mention any sort of Portuguese heritage at all. In fact, one descendent tells me that Edwards was definitely not Portuguese, and he did not have dark OR curly hair.[11] The records that I have on the Edwards and Pitts line dates back to 1160 and include France, England, Virginia, North Carolina, Georgia, and Florida. If William Edwards was not Richard's biological father, then who was?

---

[10] *Deposition G.* Judson Edwards.
[11] This statement comes from a personal letter dated 15 October 1996 to Iris Williams from William Webb, descendent of William Pitts Edwards.

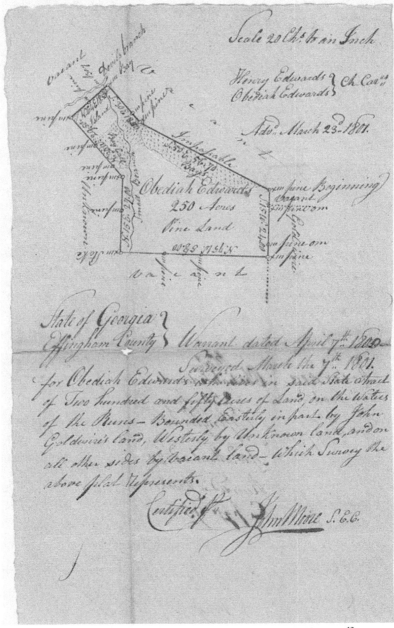

Fig. 1.4 Land Records of Obadiah Edwards' property in Springfield, GA[12]

---

[12] Land Warrant 23 Mar 1801 Effingham County Georgia Recorded in Book C, Page 95

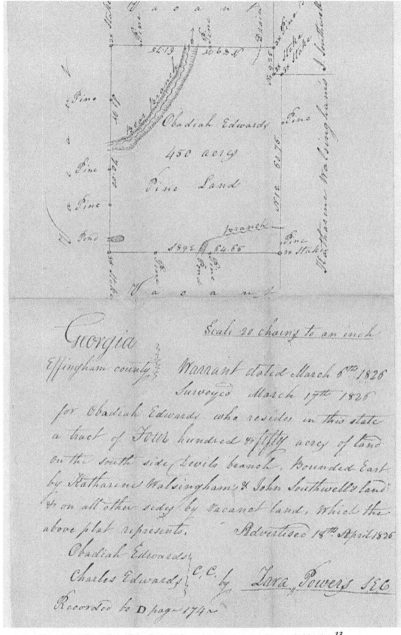

Fig. 1.5 1826 GA Obadiah Edwards' property in Springfield, GA[13]

---

[13] [13] Land Warrant 23 Mar 1801 Effingham County, Georgia Recorded in Book C, Page 95

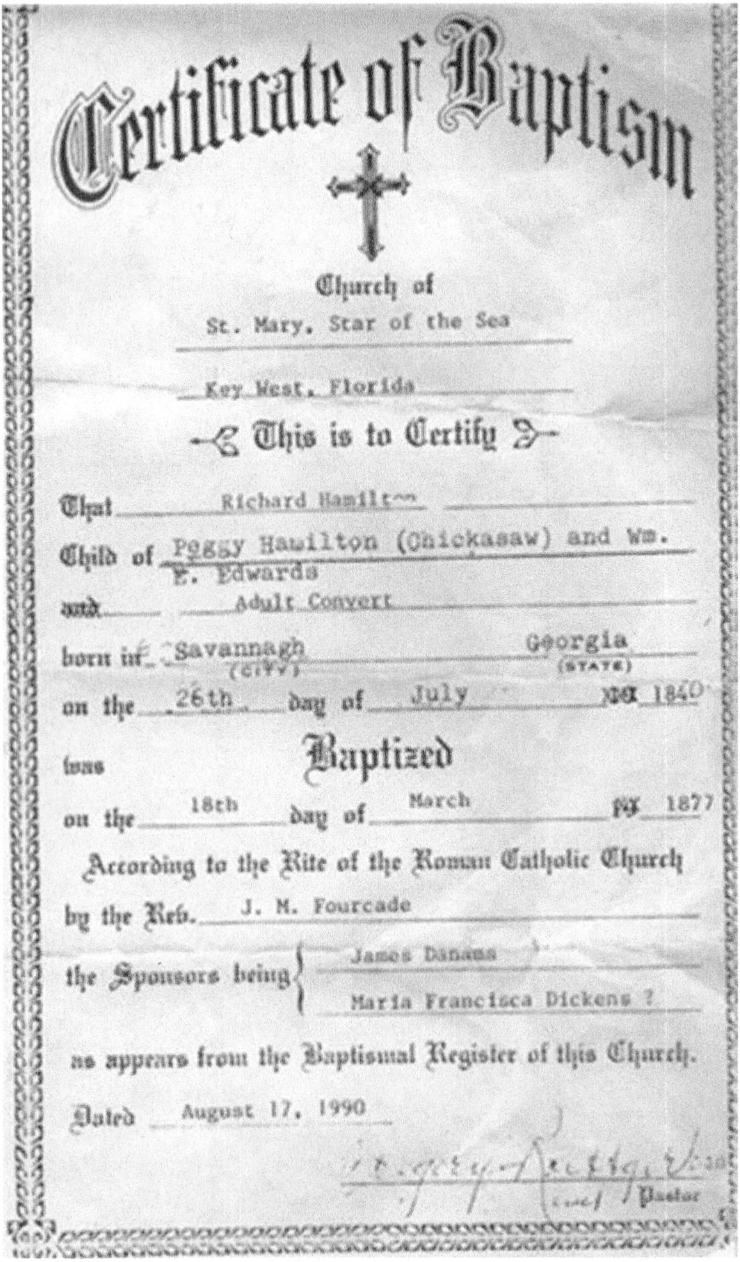

Certificate of Baptism

✝

Church of

St. Mary, Star of the Sea

Key West, Florida

~ This is to Certify ~

That Richard Hamilton

Child of Peggy Hamilton (Chickasaw) and Wm. F. Edwards

and Adult Convert

born in Savannagh (CITY) Georgia (STATE)

on the 26th day of July 18 1840

was

Baptized

on the 18th day of March 18 1877

According to the Rite of the Roman Catholic Church

by the Rev. J. M. Fourcade

the Sponsors being { James Danans

Maria Francisca Dickens ?

as appears from the Baptismal Register of this Church.

Dated August 17, 1990

Pastor

Fig. 1.7 Richard Hamilton's baptismal certificate

In several depositions, the legitimate children of Edwards state that Richard's father was a Negro slave on another plantation.

Henrietta Edwards, daughter of William Edwards, states in 1902, "I remember seeing Richard's father very well. He was a very bright mulatto and his hair was almost straight and was said to have Indian blood in his veins. I think his father was named Richard and that he belonged to Mr. Neece."[14] This corroborates Judson's description. Was Richard's version wishful thinking? Or were the other children covering for their father, not wanting to air dirty laundry?

Fig. 1.8 The only photograph of Richard as a young man

We know that Edwards came from a fairly wealthy family in Savannah. Why in the years to come his father would exclude him from his will is something we don't know. But Edwards, one of the many sons of Obadiah Edwards, was excluded and off he went in December of 1850, with his family and property, including Richard and his mother, Peggy, to the newly opened land in North Florida.

---

[14] *Deposition K.* Henrietta Edwards Jones.

Bloodlines

Richard relocated with the Edwards family and his mother to Williston, Florida, where he stayed until the Civil War broke out.

Chapter 2

CALL TO HOMESTEAD

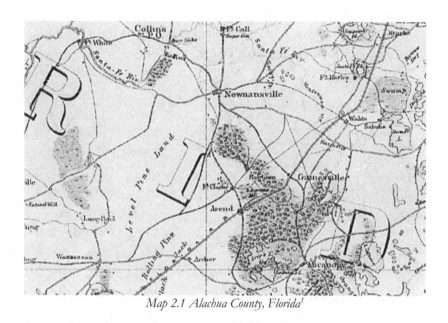

Map 2.1 Alachua County, Florida[1]

1850 - 1865 Williston, Marion County, Florida

As the Second Seminole War sank into memory and the history books, the United States government decided to find a way to populate the now mostly vacant Florida landscape. They offered land grants, and many people, especially those in Georgia and South Carolina, leapt at the chance to homestead in the Florida wilderness. The terrain in

---

[1] Map Credit: Courtesy of the National Archives and Records Administration

North Florida was very similar to the terrain in parts of Georgia, South Carolina, and Alabama. The big draw was that the climate was more accommodating and the land more fertile and far cheaper. Not to mention, that to those with a thirst for new adventures, there was not much more exciting than carving out a civilization in a new, untamed land. In his 1915 book, *History of Travel in America*, Seymour Dunbar, "By the early 1850s population began to increase all over Alachua County. Settlers from Georgia and the Carolinas were attracted by the availability of farmland that was suited to the growing of cotton, corn, and vegetable crops."[2]

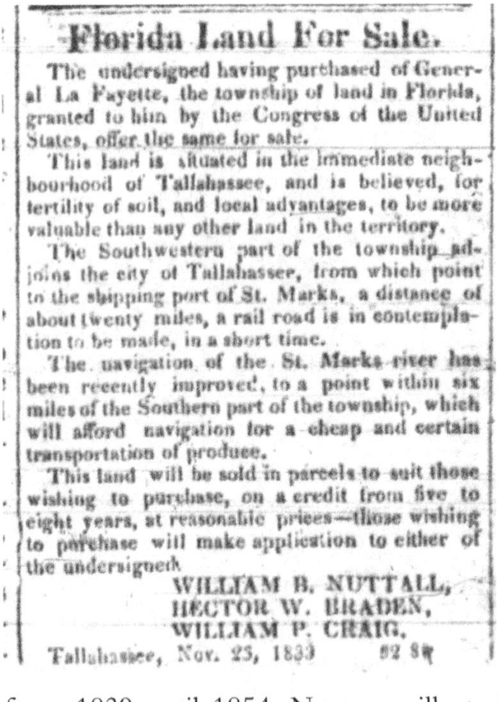

Florida Land For Sale.

The undersigned having purchased of General La Fayette, the township of land in Florida, granted to him by the Congress of the United States, offer the same for sale.

This land is situated in the immediate neighbourhood of Tallahassee, and is believed, for fertility of soil, and local advantages, to be more valuable than any other land in the territory.

The Southwestern part of the township adjoins the city of Tallahassee, from which point to the shipping port of St. Marks, a distance of about twenty miles, a rail road is in contemplation to be made, in a short time.

The navigation of the St. Marks river has been recently improved, to a point within six miles of the Southern part of the township, which will afford navigation for a cheap and certain transportation of produce.

This land will be sold in parcels to suit those wishing to purchase, on a credit from five to eight years, at reasonable prices—those wishing to purchase will make application to either of the undersigned.

WILLIAM B. NUTTALL,
HECTOR W. BRADEN,
WILLIAM P. CRAIG.

Tallahassee, Nov. 25, 1833   52 St

Fig. 2.1 Land for Sale Poster[3]

Henrietta says, "We moved to Florida in Dec 1850 and have lived right on this place until 1871."[4] They acquired some property in Newnansville, the county seat of Alachua County from 1839 until 1854. Newnansville today is a ghost town, nothing remaining but a small cemetery. In addition to the

---

[2] Dunbar, *History of Travel in America,* 1105

[3] "Florida Land for Sale." Page 3

[4] *Deposition K.* Henrietta Edwards Jones.

Newnansville property, Edwards owned three properties in Williston, Levy County, Florida, approximately 20 miles south of Gainesville.

In late 1850, when the Edwards' family made the move to Florida, Edwards and his wife had eight children ranging in age from 18 to 2. A ninth child, Laura, had recently died at the age of 7 before the move. Their 10th child, Joseph Newton would be born in Florida in the coming year, which settled the question in my mind as to whether Edwards' wife, Eleanor Southwell, actually made this trip at that time. She did arrive at some point in 1851, likely traversing the same route Edwards would travel.

Edwards was 39 years old when he joined the exodus to the new frontier. He was a farmer and had plans to turn his new properties into money makers. By 1860 he owned $5,000 in real estate, and his personal estate was worth $20,000.

We don't know what route the Edwards' family took to get to their new farm, but I was able to imagine a few scenarios. The trip from Savannah to Jacksonville was 234 miles by steamboat.[5] This voyage took approximately 2 days.[6]

Dunbar says, "The travel conditions that prevailed throughout the eastern and middle states from about 1840 to 1850 were confusing and chaotic to anyone who had purchased his knowledge at the cost of experience. There were so many different methods of making any contemplated journey of length, and so many possible conditions to be encountered during its progress that the prospective traveller (sic) was often bewildered---despite the advice he received and the innumerable guide books he read---with regard to the most desirable plan to pursue in reaching his intended destination."[7]

---

[5] Gorton, Gary. *Ante Bellum Transportation Indices, 26*
[6] Warner, I. W. *The Immigrant's Guide and Citizen's Manual.*
[7] Dunbar, Seymour. *History of Travel in America*, 1915.

Another family traveling this same route to Ocala wrote in records that they traveled down the Savannah River by boat to Jacksonville. From there they had to cross the St. John's River. They recorded that the stock was brought overland. If the Edwards' family chose to travel in a similar fashion, they would then have to first cross the St. John's River before traveling by horse and wagon from Jacksonville to the interior of the state, to Williston. The stage route was shorter by 100 miles, but undoubtedly took much longer. There was also a stage route from Savannah to Jacksonville.[8] In order to continue travel from Jacksonville, regardless of whether they traveled from Savannah by steamboat or stage route, they would still have had to cross the St. John's River to reach Newnansville, a distance of approximately 75 miles.

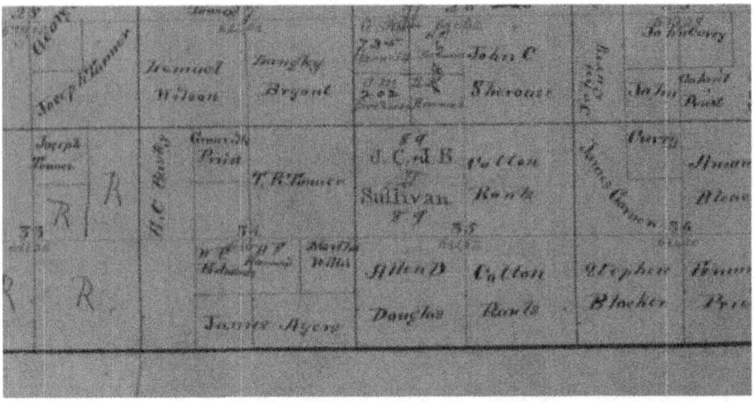

Fig. 2.2 Land Records Newnansville, Florida, 1852

---

8 Burr. *Disturnell's new map of the United States*, 1851.

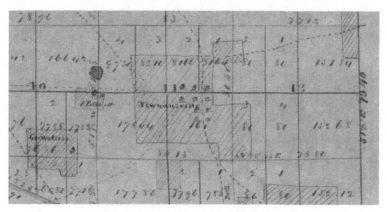

Fig. 2.3 Land Records Newnansville, Florida, 1852

They would then travel south to Micanopy where the stage route ended. From Micanopy to Williston would have involved covering 16 miles of barely recognizable and unmapped trails. All of this distance and time while transporting an entire household of goods, animals, family, and slaves through a wilderness of wildlife, unfamiliar flora, and the dangerous possibility of encountering an Indian or two. The quiet must have been unsettling. Out there in the Florida frontier, far from the nearest town or fort, the only sounds in the night were the rustling of leaves as unknown animals moved through the brush. Many a pioneer reported that they felt as if they were being watched constantly – by animals and by Indians.

The family had more to deal with in their new home than just settling in. Within five years of arriving in Williston, the Third Seminole War began. Starting in 1817, the US had evicted more than 3000 Seminoles from Florida territories by the 1850s. In 1855, the final showdown began with Billy Bowlegs and US troops. While the remaining Seminoles had tried to live peaceably in the southern half of the state, a confrontation was inevitable. When surveyors encroached into Indian territory destroying their crops, Bowlegs had had enough. Many battles ensued. For three years, the Seminoles held out against US troops before Bowlegs finally surrendered on May 7, 1858.[9]

When Edwards arrived in Williston, Florida, he had five slaves and 160 acres. Two of those slaves were Peggy and her son, Richard. During Richard's time there, from 1850 to 1865, the town was home to quite a few pioneer farmers. Edwards concentrated on farming but did own some cattle and sheep. He and his wife, Eleanor, had 75 head of cows and a pleasure carriage. By 1861 Edwards had 640 acres, 14 slaves, 275 head of cattle, and nine horses, so he must have been doing well in his new home. He was known to family and close friends as 'Uncle Billy.' The slaves called him 'Cap'n Billy.' The names of some of his slaves were Hamp, Preston, James, Ellick, Jerry, Sophia, and Sarah. Judson Edwards says, "My father owned Hamp Hamilton, Ellick Adams, Preston Hamilton, Jim Morrison, and Richard."

From this information, we learned that there were other Hamiltons owned by Edwards. Judson doesn't mention how old these other slaves were in relation to Richard.[10] Were they related to him? At any rate, from this information, I am running on the assumption that Richard had the name Hamilton while still a slave. Which means that he did not give it to himself after Emancipation as many slaves did then. When the slaves were freed, they were able to legally choose a name for themselves and their family. While some did take the name of their owners, many chose names solely on someone they had liked. I do not believe this is the case with Richard. Somehow, the name Hamilton was a part of his identity before the war ended.

In 1860 Florida, Leon County had the highest number of slaves in the state. Marion County came in second with just

---

[9] The Seminole Wars. Seminole Nation Museum.
[10] *Deposition I.* Joseph Edwards.

over half the population being slaves.[11] By the time Civil War threatened, Edwards' land holdings spread across Williston to include almost 800 acres. Records show he owned 1050 head of cattle and 12 horses. In those golden years, he was reporting 200 sheep each year. In addition to cattle, hogs, and sheep, he farmed.

Eleanor did not live to enjoy this prosperity. At age 49, in December 1861, she passed away and was buried in the family cemetery. That cemetery is still located just southwest of Fairfield, owned by Edwards descendants. One of the descendants offered to take me there, but somehow it just didn't feel right. Edwards then married Harriet Hasseltine Mixson Calhoun.

Fig. 2.4 Believed to be Eleanor Edwards

I visited two of the sites in Williston and was amazed at the abundance of old oaks, complete with moss that reached to the ground hanging from their branches. In 2018, at the time of this visit, the land was largely rolling hills of green pasture with only a few structures tucked under the trees. Cows and horses grazed the pastures. It was quiet except for the occasional car traveling Highway 316, which connects with Highway 27 there. I removed my shoes and stood barefoot on the side of the road, listening to the crickets humming, the

---

[11] Map. Image Archives of the Historical Map & Chart Collection.

horses snorting here and there, and the breeze blowing through the oak trees. I watched the clouds float by and tried to imagine Peggy and Richard walking on this very ground.

By 1891, William Arnold wrote in his travel guide, *Winter in Summerland*, that Williston is "in the midst of good phosphate and timber lands." The only listing he has for lodgings there is "private board by J. B. Epperson, who will rent out a room for $1.50 per day, special by the week or month. He can only accommodate 10 people at a time."[12]

This town is where Richard Hamilton spent his teen years. He would have been a child when he arrived, and he stayed in Williston until the end of the Civil War. Only about 25 when he left Williston, he headed for Key West. What got Key West in his head? He'd never left the farm, other than a few stints as a cook for his master's sons, they serving for the Confederate Army in Tallahassee.

During the war, he reportedly followed the Edwards boys into the Confederate Army to cook. Joseph Edwards, son of William Edwards says, "I know my brothers John and A. J. Edwards were in the confederate armies. I know that Richard was right here on this place most of the time during the war, except when he was cooking for my brothers. I saw him in camp with them, he and I went there together once and I left him there with them."[13]

Again, I infer that Richard may have grown up near his mother in the house. Perhaps Peggy was a cook in the kitchen, and that is how Richard was chosen by the brothers to serve as cook for them while they were in the Army. It was not uncommon for Confederate soldiers to take their slaves with them to the battlefield. Not every Confederate owned slaves, many could not afford to own land or slaves, but the Edwards boys were not poor, and they certainly were not accustomed to

---

[12] Arnold, William E. *Summer in the Winter Time.*
[13] *Deposition I.* Joseph Edwards.

fending for themselves. If Richard grew up as a house slave, he would be the perfect choice to take along on such a venture. He was young, strong, and not likely to run off since he was not a field slave.

Fig. 2.5 Edwards' homestead in Williston, Florida, 2018.

Although Richard would later claim that he'd served for the Union Army, the evidence supports that he did not. He filed for a military pension in 1901 under the name Stephen Barrett, a black man who served for the Union army as a private in Company C, 99 Regiment of US Colored Infantry, that was a move that backfired on Richard and would eventually send him into hiding in the Ten Thousand Islands as a fugitive.

Lincoln's Emancipation Proclamation came in 1863, but the slaves in Florida did not gain their freedom until after the Civil War ended in 1865. Yet Richard stayed in Williston according to some sources, on that farm for two and a half more years. What must that be like? To be in one family, one 'home' for 20+ years and then have the cage opened? Do you approach that open door with a mix of elation and terror? Step out of the door, fly out of the cage, or shrink back to the safety of the only home you've ever known?

The reconstruction years were difficult for everyone. Former slaves now struck out on their own, taking the trades they had learned and their knowledge of farming to attempt to forge a life for themselves and their families elsewhere. Former masters hired their former slaves to stay on and continue working for them for wages, which brought with it even more problems. Union soldiers were everywhere, trying to convince the slaves that they could leave, they were free. And yet many stayed.

In 1866, the opinion of the majority of the south was still very much against the Negro and most thought "the Negro is an alien enemy to be avoided in the great business and purposes of life."[14] Florida was especially resistant to embracing emancipation. An anonymous writer to *The Florida Peninsula* newspaper expressed the opinion that the former slaves should be removed from the nation just as the Indians had been removed, "...we know it to be the sincere wish of the entire population (the Bureau excepted)[15] that the whole race was transferred back to their native Africa. The two races will never live in harmony and all sensible men know that their destiny will be that of the red men of the forest. Indolence and a want of thrift will fix the fact beyond controversy." [16]

Imagine what it must have been like for a young man during those years. Adolescents are by nature itching to get out from under their parent's gaze, bursting to get away from the familiar and explore the unknown, sure in the knowledge that they are invincible. But Richard was a slave, so add in the urge to be free, as surely almost all of the slaves felt. As a young man at the end of the war, there would not have been much about staying on the farm that would have been attractive to

---

[14] "The Future of South Florida," p. 3
[15] Referring to the Freedmen's Bureau. This agency was created after Emancipation to help the freed slaves begin new lives. The Bureau helped them with jobs, places to live, education, legal matters, and other necessities of adapting to surviving and building a life as free people.
[15] "The Future of South Florida," p. 3
[16] Ibid.

Richard. He had a taste of life outside the farm during the war and now faced racism and a depressing life of farming that yielded scarcely more than he had as a slave. The lure of the sea and setting out as a free man must have been exciting. Richard finally left and by most accounts went to Key West. He was barely 25 years old, a young man with the world suddenly burst wide open around him.

We do know that Richard corresponded with his mother over the years after he left. Henrietta tells us in a deposition, "Richard never came back here, but I read one or two letters that he wrote back to his mother."[17] Later, after traveling around a bit, he wrote to his mother in Williston for money to return 'home.' We don't know what her answer is, but we do know that Richard never did return to Williston.

---

[17] *Deposition K.* Henrietta Edwards Jones.

Obadiah Edwards 1777-1857 --- Tabitha Pitts 1782-1863

William Pitts Edwards 1811-1887 --- Eleanor Southwell 1812-1861

Ann Haseltine b. 1832
Elvira Amanda Lee b. 1834
Adoniram Judson b. 1836
Frances Julia b. 1838
John Southwell b. 1839
Eliza Burton b. 1841
Laura K b. 1843
Henrietta b. 1845
George William b. 1848
Joseph Newton b. 1851

William Pitts Edwards --- Peggy Hamilton (slave)

Richard Edward Hamilton[18]

---

[18] There is some disagreement regarding Richard's middle name. Richard himself alternately claims that his middle name is Edward or Eugene. There is no dispute that he was often referred to as simply R. E. Hamilton.

Chapter 3

MISSING YEARS

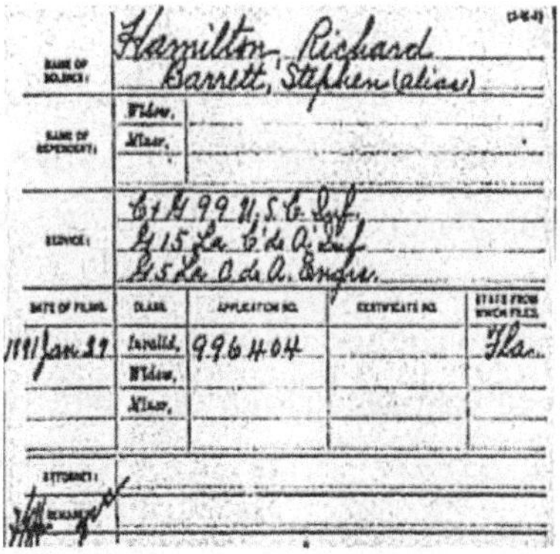
NAME OF SOLDIER: Hamilton, Richard
Barrett, Stephen (alias)
NAME OF DEPENDENT: Widow, Minor,
SERVICE: C & G 99 U.S.C. Inf.
G 15 La. C'de A. Inf.
G 5 La. C de A. Engrs.

DATE OF FILING.	CLASS.	APPLICATION NO.	CERTIFICATE NO.	STATE FROM WHICH FILED.
1891 Jan. 29	Invalid,	996404		Fla.
	Widow,			
	Minor,			

ATTORNEY:
REMARKS:

Figure 3.1 Barrett case folder cover

The majority of the research on Peggy Hamilton, Richard Hamilton, and William Pitts Edwards stems from a case filed in January 1891 by Richard Hamilton requesting pension for serving in the Civil War. In this request, Richard used the name Stephen Barrett. A flurry of depositions was taken to determine if Richard Hamilton, alias Stephen Barrett, actually served in the war. I was able to glean much personal information about my ancestors from these documents but none of them that I can call facts.

Richard maintains that he enlisted in the US Colored Troops at Pleasunth (sic) Hill, Louisiana in late 1862 or early 1863. He claims his captain's name was John Moore. He claims he did so under the name of Stephen Barrett. Richard was later arrested for filing for pension under this name, as there was also a claim filed by the real Stephen Barrett's widow, Sarah Barrett. Hamilton descendants say that Richard and Stephen were good friends, although this is not substantiated by any evidence that I have found.

In November 1866, Stephen Barrett filed a claim for back pay from his service in Company C, 99th Regiment of the U. S. Colored Infantry under the command of Captain Frank Harding. In Barrett's claim, he states that he volunteered in New Orleans the summer of 1863 and was honorably discharged in Tallahassee the spring of 1866. The claim was filed in New Orleans. Shortly thereafter, Sarah filed for a widow's pension. This claim kicked off an investigation into the 1866 claim. In early 1898, the special examiner sent a report to the government stating, "First: That the invalid claimant (referring to Richard) is an imposter. Second: That the widow lived with the genuine soldier as his wife for a number of years without the form of marriage ceremony, which, in fact, would have been invalid, anyway, as she has a husband now living, from whom she has never been divorced."

But the investigation did not end there. In October 1901, another claim was filed in Key West by Richard Hamilton, alias Stephen Barrett, asking for "arrears of pay, travel pay, allowances, or bounty due for said services." Both applications were signed by the claimant with an X. Joseph and Henrietta Edwards both claim that Richard's only service in the Army was as a cook for their brothers, John and Judson, in the Confederate Army.

Henrietta: "I was at home all during the war. I remember that Richard was here only when he was with my brothers John and A.J. Edwards. They were both in the Confederate service in the 2nd Cav. I know that my brother John never went to New Orleans. My brother John joined the Army in Sept 1861 and before that he was here. After he joined the Army, he never left the State. I remember well that Richard was here at the close of the war and that he did not leave here until after my brothers came out of the Army. They came home in May and Richard did not leave before June, or July I know. Richard never came back here."[1]

In any case, an investigation ensued and to this day it has not been determined whether or not Richard, alias Stephen Barrett, was ever in the army at all. The case was rejected in November 1899 because it was determined that it could not be proven that "he was identical with the soldier who rendered the service."

"...had this man ever gone and served for this country as a soldier he would have one redeeming feature in his (life) to have commanded my sympathy," says G. H. Watson, of the dry goods store in Everglade[2] to J. A. Davis, chief pension examiner in 1902. He obviously did not believe Richard's story either. One of the pages in the packet of depositions includes a list of every deponent and what their reputation was. Each deponent is listed as 'Excellent' or 'Good.' Richard's reputation? 'Bad.'

Accounts from Richard's acquaintances during the pension case offer a brief glimpse into Richard's character. "He claims Everglade Fla.," states J. M. Phipps an attorney, in a deposition taken December 11, 1901, "as his post office, but I have been informed that he spends only a part of his time at that place, and the remainder of his time he is in Key West, he seems to be sort of a farmer and coal burner, on the little islands near the post office Everglade." Mr. Phipps goes on to add to his own opinion of Richard, who he knows only by the name Barrett, "Barrett is a very stupid and ignorant Negro, and his memory as to past events is exceedingly defective." Phipps insists, "from reliable information I learned that he (Richard)

---

[1] *Deposition K.* Henrietta Edwards Jones.
[2] Everglades City

came to Key West, a few years after the close of the Civil War, and has been here and on the Florida Keys ever since."[3]

There actually was a Stephen Barrett who served in the Civil War and he was most certainly not Richard Hamilton. Depositions taken by many people show that Richard was known by one name or the other. Richard claims, "There is one man in Key West named John Fletcher who knows me by both names. He did not know me in the Army. There is no person on earth who knows me by both names. I could not give you any name of any person who knew me as Stephen Barrett."[4] In that one short exchange, we can see how Richard changes his story. He claims there is one person who knows him by both names, and then immediately after says no one knows him by both names. U. S. Marshall F. W. Johnson states in November 1902, "I had known him as Richard Hamilton a good many years. I remember being called in as a witness to attest his mark when he made his application. I identified him as Stephen Barrett, on his say so. I knew him as Hamilton. I saw Hamilton make his mark as Stephen Barrett."[5]

Family members report that Richard Hamilton was a kind, loving man and acted as a midwife within the 'lower classes' of Island society. Mary Hamilton Clark states in a newspaper article in 1990 that "He (Richard Hamilton) was wonderful. My mother said he was the most loving man she had ever known. I was only 4 1/2 when he died, but I can remember I would sit on his lap, and we were shelling peas. He would say why don't you taste them. He and I were sitting there eating raw peas."[6]

The issue of Richard's race was an important one during the case because the examiners were trying to match up the

---

[3] Phipps, J. M. Attorney at Law, Key West. Letter to Hon. H. Clay Evins, Commissioner of Pensions.

[4] *Deposition D.* Hamilton, Richard.

[5] *Deposition O.* F. W. Johnson. 18 November 1902. Case of Stephen Barrett.

[6] Rogers, Bill. "Novel tarnishes woman's cherished memories."

physical descriptions. All interviewed agreed that Stephen Barrett was without a doubt a black man, married to a black wife. Richard's description is more colorful. He is described as mulatto, octoroon, and black, depending on the deponent.

Joseph Pinckney, in an 1896 deposition describes Richard as "…very tall, I judge six feet or over, a rawboned man. He is a copper colored man, looks like he might have Indian blood in him, and his hair is black and pretty straight, and he wears a heavy mustache. He has a little curious walk, he is not a crippled man, but he has some defect in his walk. He is a little bowlegged."

Nelson English, former postmaster, paints this picture of Richard – "…he is over six feet tall, his complexion is Copper color like an Indians, black and nearly straight hair, he looks like a Creole French like some of those Louisianians and he wears a mustache."[7]

Another deponent who served with Stephen Barrett describes Barrett as 50 years old, a few inches over five feet, and "a little darker than gingercake."[8]

In the summary report, the acting commissioner states, "The genuine soldier (Barrett) according to this discharge certificate and according to the records of the War Department was 25 years of age at the time he enlisted, August 20, 1863; was five feet, six inches high and was black--in every respect an African. The contesting invalid claimant, Richard Hamilton, alias Stephen Barrett, of Key West, Florida, is light in color, an octoroon, over six feet tall as shown by the evidence herewith set forth was about 19 years of age in 1868 or 1869--four years after the close of the Civil War.[9] As the years rolled into the

---

[7] *Deposition A.* Nelson English.

[8] *Deposition B.* Isom Anthony.

[9] Summary Report. Case of Stephen Barrett and Sarah Barrett.

mid-1900s, Richard was listed as white on the U.S. census rolls.[10]

Just before Christmas in 1901, a letter was sent to the Pension Bureau stating that Special Examiner Davis had returned all papers and stated "that it was impossible for him to locate the claimant, Stephen Barrett; that the place where he lives is very inaccessible, requiring a sailboat trip from Key West eight or ten miles distant; that the claimant was a fugitive from justice for violation of the Florida laws, and that he, the Special Examiner, doubted whether he could be able to secure a sworn statement from the claimant, even though he could approach his home, as the marshals and other constabulary officers of the State of Florida had frequently attempted to cause the claimant's arrest, without success."[11]

Special Examiner Davis was finally able to meet with Richard for a brief interview in Key West. Below is a transcription of that interview with Richard in 1902. I am including it in its entirety because it is Richard 'speaking.' In this interview, the reader can get a bit of Richard's personality. It is obvious here that he is lying about many things. He claims to not know the other slaves who worked on the Edwards plantation in Williston, hardly likely that he would not know them, especially since two of them shared his last name. He also claims to not know Lou Anderson, a man his mother was married to since before coming to Florida in 1850.

DEPOSITION E: Richard Hamilton

"Case of Stephen Barrett, No. 996.404

On this seventeenth day of November 1902, at Key West, county of Monroe State of Florida, before me, JA Davis, a

---

[10] Summary Report. Case of Stephen Barrett and Sarah Barrett.
[11] Legal files of Barrett case, C43 12/23/1901

special examiner of the Bureau of Pensions, personally appeared Stephen Barrett alias Richard Hamilton, who, being by me first duly sworn to answer truly all interrogatories propounded to him during this special examination of aforesaid claim for pension, deposes and says:

I am the identical person who made a statement before you last month, at St (Josephs) Island, relating to my claim for a pension.

Q. You swore that you were a soldier in Co. G 99th Regt. U.S.C. Troops enlisted the last of 1862, or first of 1863, is that correct?

A. That is right, that is correct.

Q. You stated that you were a son of Wm Edwards and that you went with a half-brother, John Edwards, to New Orleans, La. during the war, is that correct?

A. Yes sir, I did that.

Q. Was John a son of Wm Edwards?

A. Yes sir, he is dead and gone now and there is no one to say whether it is so, or not.

Q. Did you have any other half-brothers?

A. Yes sir, Joseph and Judson Edwards. Joseph was living the last time I heard anything, and Judson went crazy.

Q. Did you ever go back to Mr. Edwards after you left in 1862?

A. I never went back there after I left them in 1862 or 1863.

Q. You were never there after the war?

A. No sir, I never appeared to none of them.

Q. Do you know whether any of your half-brothers were in the Confederate Army?

A. Yes sir, two of them, John and Judson.

Q. Is this the same John who went with you to New Orleans?

A. Yes sir.

Q. He did not enlist in the Union Army?

A. No sir.

Q. Were you ever in the Confederate Army?

A. No sir.

Q. Did you ever go with John or Judson as cook?

A. No sir.

Q. Is your mother's name Peggy Anderson?

A. She goes by the name Anderson now, but I don't know her husband.

Q. Did you ever know Abram (?) Brooks?

A. No sir. I knew a man here named Irving (?) Brooks. I do not know where he came from.

Q. Did you ever know Preston Hamilton?

A. No sir.

Q. Did you ever know Ellick Adams, or Jim Morrison?

A. No sir, I don't know them.

Q. Didn't they used to belong to Wm Edwards?

A. I don't know — you got me kind of bothered.

Q. Have you got a sister living?

A. Never that I knew of.

Q. Did you ever have any sisters?

A. Never that I knew of.

Q. Did you ever know C.C. Rawls?

A. No sir. I beg your pardon I knew a Wm Rawls after I went to Manatee Co, but I knew them after I went there in 1868, or 1869.

Q. Who made out your application for a pension?

A. The last one was made out by Mr. Phipps.

Q. You (was) sworn to it before Mr. Phipps?

A. Yes sir, I testified before him that I belonged to the 99th Regt. I told him that I could prove I was in the 99th Regt.

Q. You signed that application Stephen Barrett, by mark?

A. Yes sir.

Q. Who mailed the paper to Washington?

A. I left it with Judge Phipps to mail.

Q. What were the names of your half-sisters?

Missing Years

A. Eliza, Ann, Henrietta and (Frances).

Q. Did you have a sister named Matilda?

A. I don't know any such person.

I have fully understood your questions. My answers have been correctly recorded.

Geo. G. Brooks of Key West Fla., hereby certify that the written deposition was read to deponent, that he signed the same by mark, was sworn to in my ----

Geo. G. Brooks

Stephen X (his mark) Barrett alias Richard Hamilton.

Deponent.

Sworn to and subscribed before me this 17th day of November 1902, and I certify that the contents were fully made known to deponent before signing.

JA Davis

Special Examiner

Later in the same year, Special Examiner Davis tried once again to reach Richard. He wrote to Richard, "I wish you would inform me just how far and in which direction you reside from Everglades, as, in the (event) of our failure to meet, I could send you word, and be able to find you when I am in at Everglade."[12]

---

[12] Legal files, C17 02/10/1902

The Attorney General recommended that criminal proceedings against Richard Hamilton be brought "unless good and sufficient reason for not doing so."[13] While an indictment for fraud was finally brought against Richard in May 1903, the acting District Attorney reported that he could not try the case because "the Marshal has not been able to locate and arrest the defendant." Furthermore, the acting commissioner added that "It is understood that this man (Richard) resides on a small island, some distance from Key West, and in a very inaccessible location."[14]

By 1904 the attorneys and examiners were satisfied that "the genuine Stephen Barrett is dead, and that Richard Hamilton did not serve as alleged under the name of Stephen Barrett, nor was he otherwise in the military service of the U. S."[15]

Ultimately, it was decided that it was too time consuming and expensive to continue searching for Richard Hamilton in the Ten Thousand Islands and the case was nolle prossed in June 1920 by the United States Attorney, and Richard disappeared into the Florida Everglades.

---

[13] Legal files of Barrett case, C163 02/02/1903
[14] Legal files of Barrett Case, C4
[15] Legal files of Barrett Case, C3 06/23/1904

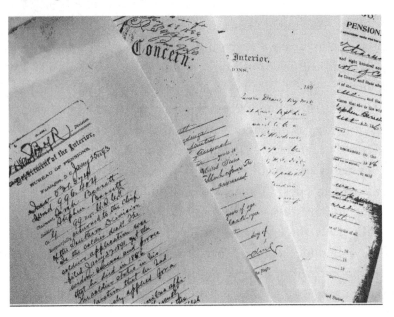

The Case of Stephen Barrett: Transcription of Summary Report[16]

3-1868

LAW DIVISION

Department of the Interior,

Bureau of Pensions,

Washington, D. C. January 24, 1903.

The Honorable,

The Secretary of the Interior.

Sir:

I herewith have the honor to forward the original papers in the claims of Stephen Barrett, alleged late private, Cos. C and G, 99th U. S. C. V. I., Orig. No. 996,404, and of Sarah Barrett, alleging that her deceased husband is the identical person who rendered said service, Orig. No. 531,374, together with reports of Special Examiners Davis, Wiggenhorn, Montgomery and Gilpin relative thereto, for your consideration and reference to the Department of Justice, for transmission to the United States Attorney for the Southern District of Florida, with a view to the criminal prosecution of the invalid claimant, Stephen Barrett, whose genuine name is Richard Hamilton, and whose post office address is Key West, Monroe County, Florida, c/o John A. Pitcher, but who actually resides, however some forty miles north of Key West upon one of the Island Keys, known as the Ten Thousand Isles, for violation of the

---

[16] *Summary Report*. Case of Stephen Barrett and Sarah Barrett.

provisions of section 5438, Revised Statutes of the United States.

HISTORY.

The invalid claimant, Richard Hamilton, alias Stephen Barrett, first filed a declaration January 27, 1891. This claim was rejected November 26, 1899, on the ground that he failed to prove that he was identical with the soldier who rendered the service. The widow claimant filed her claim November 6, 1891, and a second declaration December 3, 1896. Her claim was rejected August 12, 1899, upon the ground that she was not the legal widow of the deceased soldier, having a living husband from whom she was not divorced at the time of the soldier's death.

The widow claimant, Sarah Barrett, whose real name is Sarah Miller, did live for many years with the soldier as his wife, though she, as herinbefore stated, had a living husband from whom she was not divorced throughout the entire period of her association with the soldier. Among other papers filed by her is the original discharge certificate granted to the soldier of this service, and which was in the possession of the said Stephen Barrett, with whom she lived as his wife at the time of his death, which had been in his possession constantly after his discharge from the service. The genuine soldier according to this discharge certificate and according to the records of the War Department was 25 years of age at the time he enlisted, August 20, 1863; was five feet, six inches high and was black-- in every respect an African. The contesting invalid claimant, Richard Hamilton, alias Stephen Barrett, of Key West, Florida, is light in color, an octoroon, over six feet tall as shown by the evidence herewith set forth was about 19 years of age in 1868 or 1869--four years after the close of the civil war.

The evidence upon which this recommendation is based is briefly set forth as follows:

Isom Anthony, of Killona, Saint Charles Parish, Louisiana, in a deposition before Special Examiner J. W. Montgomery, states that he served in Cos. H and C, 99th U.S.C.V.I.; that he was acquainted with one Stephen Barrett, who served in Cos. G and C of the same regiment; that deponent met him in said service; that the said Barrett was about five feet, six inches tall, was black in color, with black hair and eyes and weighed about one hundred and fifty pounds; was fully grown; that deponent and the said Stephen Barrett settled in Saint Charles Parish after service and deponent knew him well from that time until the time of his death; that at the time of his death he was living with a woman by the name of Sarah as his wife.

Exhibit 3, page 23, of the report of Special Examiner A. C. Wiggenhorn, is the original discharge certificate granted by Captain Frank D. Harding to Stephen Barrett as a member of Co. C, setting forth the fact that he was duly enlisted in said company of the 99th U.S.C.V.I., on the 20th day of August, 1863, and honorably discharged therefrom on April 23, 1866, at Tallahassee, Florida--services being no longer required; that he was born in Virginia, was 25 years of age at the time of enlistment; five feet, six inches high, with black complexion, black eyes, and black hair.

The records of the War Department show that there was but one soldier by the name Stephen Barrett who rendered service in Companies C and G, 99th U. S. C. V. I.; that he was mustered into Co, G, 99th U.S.C.V.I., August 20, 1863, and mustered out April 23, 1866, as of Co. C, said Reg., to which he was transferred December 8, 1865.

Special Examiner J. A. Davis, who may be addressed Commissioner of Pensions, Washington, D.C., is competent to testify that on the 18th day of October, 1902, Richard Hamilton, alias Stephen Barrett, the original invalid claimant for pension as member of Cos. C and G, 99th U.S.C.V.I., stated to him that the claimant was a slave; that he was born in Savannah, Georgia; that his mother was named Peggy Hamilton, owned by one William Edwards who was claimant's father; that the said William Edwards moved from Savannah, Georgia, to Marion County, Florida, together with his family and his slaves, including the claimant, Richard Hamilton, alias Stephen Barrett; that the said William Edwards had several children, John, Joseph and Judson; that John is dead; Judson is crazy and Joseph is living somewhere in Florida; that claimant, Richard Hamilton, alias Stephen Barrett, in 1863, left the home of William Edwards, in Marion County, Florida, together with his half-brother, John Edwards and proceeded to Louisiana where the claimant enlisted in Co. G, 99th U.S.C.V.I., and served in the same until he was transferred to Co. C, and discharged therefrom.

Judson Edwards, of Ocala, Marion County, Florida, before Special Examiner Davis states that he is the son of William Edwards, who resided in Marion County, Florida for many years before his death; that deponent's father prior to 1850, when he came to Marion County, Florida, lived in Savannah, Georgia; that among other slaves owned by him was one Richard Hamilton, who was born in Savannah in July, 1848; that Richard Hamilton's mother was named Peggy and she was also owned by deponent's father; that Richard Hamilton remained with deponent's father until the spring of 1865; that deponent served in the Confederate army, in the 2d Florida Calvary, but did not leave the State of Florida and was at home frequently during his service in said organization and that the boy, Richard Hamilton, was throughout the entire period upon deponent's father's place in Marion County, Florida, with the exception of a short while when he cooked for deponent and his brother John, who was also a member of the 2d Florida Cavalry, Confederate States Army; that he did not leave the farm of deponent's father until sometime in May, 1865-- deponent thinks the 19th day of that month; that deponent remembers distinctly incidents connected with the morning that the said Richard Hamilton left his father's home; that the said Richard Hamilton went to Key West, Florida, where he has continued to reside ever since; that some years after he left deponent's father, he received a letter from Richard Hamilton, begging that money be sent him to come back to Marion County, Florida, stating that he desired to come there and live; that Richard Hamilton's mother, Peggy Hamilton, lived upon the place of deponent' father until the day of her death and was buried by deponent's family; that deponent's brother John was never in the State of Louisiana in his life, nor was Richard Hamilton ever in said State until after May, 1865, and not then to the knowledge of deponent; that said Richard Hamilton was never known as Stephen Barrett to deponent's knowledge and was never a member of the Federal army or navy; that he was never old enough to have been a member of either during the war.

Ellick Anderson, of Elmwood, Marion County, Florida, in a deposition before Special Examiner Davis, states that he is well acquainted with Richard Hamilton, who belonged as a slave to one William Edwards, who lived in Savannah, Georgia, until 1850, when he moved to Marion County, Florida and lived until the day of his death; that deponent is an uncle of the said Richard Hamilton; that the said Richard Hamilton is a son of Peggy Hamilton, who was also a slave of Mr. William Edwards; that Richard Hamilton, at the time of the Civil War was nothing but a boy; that he was not absent from William Edwards' place in Marion County, Florida, for any period whatsoever, other than a short time that he was cooking for William Edwards' two sons, John and A. J. Edwards, who were Confederate soldiers in a Florida organization, which did not leave the State; that Richard Hamilton did not leave Marion County, Florida, other than to cook for the aforesaid John and A. J. Edwards, until after May 1865.

Joseph Edwards of Elmwood, Marion County, Florida, in a deposition before Special Examiner Davis, states that he is a son of William Edwards; that he had brothers by the name of John and Judson Edwards and a sister by the name of Henrietta; that deponent's father, prior to 1850, lived in Savannah, Georgia, and owned slaves, among whom were Peggy Hamilton and a son of hers, Richard by name; that Richard and Peggy Hamilton were brought by members of the family to Marion County, Florida, and Peggy lived with the family until the day of her death, several years ago; that Richard Hamilton was nothing more than a boy during the Civil War and was not absent from deponent's father's place, in Marion County, Florida, during the Civil War or any time whatsoever other than a short period, when he was cooking for deponent's brothers, John and Judson, who were members of the Confederate Cavalry organization, known as the 2d Florida, which did not go outside of the confines of the State of Florida.; deponent saw Richard Hamilton cooking for his brothers in said camp; that the said Richard Hamilton did not leave Marion County permanently until after the close of the Civil War, when he settled in Key West, Florida, and has continued to reside there since.

Henrietta E. Jones, of Elmwood, Marion County, Florida, in a deposition before Special Examiner Davis, states that she is a daughter of William Edwards, who, until 1850, resided in Savannah, Georgia, when he moved to Marion County, Florida, where he lived until the day of his death, some years ago; that the said William Edwards was possessed of several slaves--among them Peggy Hamilton, a son of hers, Richard Hamilton, born July, 1848. These two, Peggy and Richard Hamilton, were brought to Marion County, Florida, with the family, in 1850, and Peggy remained with them until the day of her death, several years ago. Richard remained with the family until he went to Key West, Florida, to live, in 1865, after the Civil War; was on the place in Marion County, Florida, throughout the entire period of the Civil War, except for a short time when he was cooking for two of deponent's brothers, John and A. Judson Edwards, who were members of the 2nd Florida Cavalry, Confederate Army; that the said Richard Hamilton was thus cooking for John and Judson Edwards but a very short time, however; that he was not a member of any Federal military organization, because he was not long enough absent from deponent's home to have been a member of any military establishment and within the short time he was absent from said home his absence was fully accounted for and his habits known by reason of the fact that he was cooking for the aforesaid John and Judson Edwards.

X x x x x x x x x x x x x x x x x x x x x x x

J. M. Phipps, of Key West, Monroe county, Florida, in a deposition before the Special Examiner Davis, states that he is an attorney-at-law and a notary public; that he is not acquainted personally with one Stephen Barrett, but that he does know by sight, a Negro man, who executed a claim for pension before deponent under the name of Stephen Barrett; that what purports to be deponent's signature to the jurat of a declaration purporting to have been executed by Stephen Barrett, October 9, 1901, in the presence of F. W. Johnson, and George G. Brooks as attesting and identifying witnesses, and filed in the Bureau of Pensions October 14, 1901, is in fact deponent's genuine signature and the paper was executed as it purports;

that said paper was prepared by deponent at the dictation of the said Stephen Barrett, after which Stephen Barrett signed the same by mark and subscribed to the oath administered to him by deponent in the presence of attesting and identifying witnesses.

George G. Brooks, of Key West, Florida, in his deposition before Special Examiner Davis, states that he is an attorney-at-law; that he has no personal acquaintance with one Stephen Barrett, but that he is well acquainted with one Richard Hamilton, a Negro who lives some miles north of Key West, on one of the Florida Island Keys; that what purports to be deponent's signature as an attesting and identifying witness to a declaration executed by Stephen Barrett, October 9, 1901, in the presence of George G. Brooks and F. W. Johnson, before J. M. Phipps, a notary public, and filed in the Bureau of Pensions, October 14, 1901, is in fact deponent's genuine signature; said paper was executed by the person deponent knows as Richard Hamilton, who alleged that his army name was Stephen Barrett.

F. W. Johnson, of Key West, Florida, in a deposition before Special Examiner Davis, states that he is Deputy United States Marshal, located in Key West; that his signature as an attesting and identifying witness to a declaration purporting execution by Stephen Barrett, before J. M. Phipps in the presence of deponent and George G. Brooks, is in fact deponent's genuine signature; that deponent does not know the claimant as Stephen Barrett at all, but does know him as Richard Hamilton; that he stated that he sought pension under the name of Stephen Barrett, because he rendered service under that name, at the time of the execution of his declaration.

Inasmuch as the Statute of Limitations prevent criminal proceedings in connection with the first declaration filed by

Richard Hamilton, alias Stephen Barrett, the proceedings herein recommended, if instituted, must be based upon the declaration executed October 9, 1901, and filed October 14, 1901. The records of this Bureau do not show the filing of any but the first declaration and there are no certified copies of record by which the actual filing of this declaration can be shown, as provided for in section 882, Revised Statutes of the United States.

In event criminal proceedings are instituted, as hereinbefore recommended, the foregoing witnesses, whose addresses have been given, or such of them as may be deemed expedient by the United States Attorney, should appear in behalf of the Government, and a subpoena duces tecum should issue addressed to the Secretary of War, directing him or some employs of that Department designated by him in his stead to produce the original roll of Companies C and G, 99th U. S. C. V. I., to show that there was but one soldier who rendered service in either of said organizations under the name Stephen Barrett and he was transferred from one organization to the other, and his personal description.

Very respectfully,

J. L. _____

Acting Commissioner.

Missing Years

Chapter 4

A NEW LIFE

Arcadia[1]
1867 - 1871

Map 4.1 Newly divided counties Manatee and DeSoto. Rand McNally 1892.

In 1863, President Lincoln spoke to the freed slaves in his famous speech, The Emancipation Proclamation, "And I hereby enjoin upon the people so declared to be free to abstain from all violence; unless in necessary self-defense: and I recommend to them that in all cases when allowed, they labor faithfully for reasonable wages." There was a very well-

---

[1] Rand McNally 1892

founded concern that the freedmen would not know how to make a living on their own. But the larger fear was for the economic safety of the South, as well as the nation, which was in danger of collapsing now that the ex-slaves were freed. In Florida, the authorities "urged the freedmen to stay with their old masters."[2]

The rumor running rampant among the freedmen was that the President had promised them all 'forty acres and a mule' to start their lives over. They quickly found out that this was not true at all. Within a year of scrabbling to survive, many of the former slaves went back to their masters to work. This created a whole new set of problems for landowners and freedmen alike. The owners had to pay wages and the freedmen had no choice but to accept very poor wages and harsh working conditions. Contract labor was the accepted solution, and that came with all the requisite abuses and very little of the promised rewards. Still, many freedmen in Florida carried on with their former owners. Peggy Hamilton and her husband, Lou Anderson, stayed near William Edwards for many years after Emancipation. Richard Hamilton, however, had had enough of servitude.

Just what Richard did after being granted his freedom is anyone's guess. He claims he went to Key West, hopped a freighter and sailed to Liverpool.[3] Others report that he stayed on at the Williston farm for 2 ½ years after being freed and then disappeared. Following his scattered trail, I found him in Manatee County married to Hannah Elizabeth Moore. They married in 1869. In just a few short years, another woman was added to this household, Mary A. Weeks, who would become Richard's wife while he was still married to Hannah.

---

[2] [2] Eckert, Edward K. Contract Labor in Florida during Reconstruction, p. 35
[3] *Deposition D*. Richard Hamilton.

The State of Florida seceded from the Union in May 1865. This secession lasted only a short time and was repealed by October of that year. Because of continued Confederate sympathies, the Peace River area was assigned a troop of Union forces to keep the peace. The 99th US Colored Troops was sent to Manatee County, but this occupation only lasted a few months.

As reconstruction from the Civil War commenced, some of Florida's former slaves migrated south, following the Peace River, to the fertile land and cattle grazing fields of Pine Level. The main industry at this time centered around citrus growing and cattle ranching. The small town was the county seat of Manatee County from 1866 until 1868 when the county seat moved southeast to Arcadia, about 11 miles from Pine Level. As the towns became more and more populated, a new county, DeSoto County, was created in 1887, with Arcadia the county seat. Much of the Peace Valley region was a wilderness at this time. The first families settled in Pine Level around 1869, right about the time that Richard and Hannah took up residence where they began farming and raising a family.

Richard at some point in 1868, arrived in Pine Level. Nathan H. DeCoster, a fruit grower in DeSoto County says he employed Richard, "from about 1867 to about 1871. I first employed him at Key West Fla., to come over here and work for us. He was a boy then about eighteen or nineteen years old, I should judge. He was a light complexion, about an Octoroon color, a smart active intelligent boy. He was about 5 ft 10 in tall, rather slim built. (His) hair was straight black hair, a little bit curly, but not kinky at all. I do not seem to remember what if any history he gave me as to where he was from, or what he had been doing…he was active, strong and rugged."[4] From DeCoster's account, depositions, and census records, we can definitively place Richard in Pine Level from 1867 to 1871.

---

[4] *Deposition.* N. H. DeCoster.

Along with Richard, three other black men are reported to have arrived in Manatee County with DeCoster: Joseph Chapman, age 40; Mitchell Harrison, age 20; and John Lomans, age 25.

While the town was founded in the 1850s, complete with courthouse, it did not become the county seat of Manatee County until April 29, 1866. Manatee County would later become the first county seat of DeSoto County when Manatee and DeSoto counties merged. This designation would only last for 18 months, as county seats had a habit of relocating wherever the new train tracks were lain, and that railway line cut through Arcadia, a mere 16 miles southeast of Pine Level.[5] By the time Richard settled in Pine Level, Arcadia had emerged as the wild west of Florida. Thieves, renegades and murderers found refuge in the vast wilderness that was also home to scores of panthers, bears, and wildcats. In 1855, Pine Level was the home of the notorious Sarasota Vigilantes' murders. The rivers and creeks contained numerous alligators. According to local historian, George Lane, Jr., "Arcadia was the place to go if you needed to hire a killer cheap."[6] Because of the lack of transportation and the sparseness of the population, crime was rampant, and the local law-enforcement had a hard time containing it. It was another place to get lost, another place where a person of mixed race could 'fit in.'

In 1870, Richard and Hannah and their baby son Thomas lived in Township 38 of Manatee County in 1870, Pine Level. All three of them are listed as black. There were 24 families living in Township 38 in 1870. All were white farmers or cattlemen with the exception of two black families living next door to one another, the Harrison's and the Hamilton's. If they were all listed as black, then we can assume that they were either black or of mixed race. If they were Native Americans,

---

[5] Works Progress Administration, Historical Records Survey.

[6] Lane, George. *A Pictorial History of Arcadia and DeSoto County.*

the census-taker would surely know the difference between an Indian and a black person. Those of mixed race were most often simply listed as Mulatto or Black. After the war ended, there were many mixed-race people trying to find their place in the world. It didn't matter if the color of their skin was white or even if they could 'pass' as white. All it took was one single white person to know you were a former slave or one tiny suspicion that you were 'other,' and you were listed as 'black.' The American government was particular about enumerating the Native American population, and they were listed on special census'. It is possible that Peggy Hamilton was mixed - Indian and Black, but every census taker from 1870 until she died listed her as black. It is interesting to note that this is the single instance I have found that listed Hannah Moore as 'black.' All other records record her as 'white.' Richard Hambleton (sic) was listed as a black juror for Manatee County in November 1868 and as a "colored" taxpayer (Richard Hamilton) on the 1868 Manatee Back Tax List.

In 1867, John Lomans served as a Voter Registrar in Manatee County. The First Reconstruction Act divided ten southern states into five military districts, including Florida. Under the Second Reconstruction Act, Florida military districts were responsible for registering voters, including the freedmen. Each district was required to appoint three men as registrars, and one of those men had to be a freedman. One military official remarked, "There is only one man in Manatee County who can read & write & none in Polk County. I can get good intelligent & practical men, but they have no education whatever."

By 1870, families were scattered across the area, most often miles from one another, and Pine Level had a post office, a jail (rudimentary courthouse) and two churches. Richard lived nearby to Mitchell Harrison, one of the other black men living in Pine Level at that time. In 1871, Richard and Mitchell had an altercation. According to circuit court records, the state had filed suit against Harrison for an altercation with John Lomans. It's not exactly clear what happened from the following transcriptions, but we can get a sense of the tone of the environment at the time from them. Lomans, Harrison, and Richard clearly did not get along.

Richard says, "...John Lomans went down there and was a scandalizing me behind my back to a stranger was what I whipped him for -- a man he did not know until then and my wife likewise he scandalized to Mitchell, good as told John Beal that I was a grand rascal and _____ his witching."

Harrison added, "John Lomans told Richard Hambleton that this man John Beall that he kept my wife ever since I was gone to Key West that's what I whipped him for..."[7]

Fig. 4.1. Author at the site of the Old Pine Level Courthouse, 2018

There is nothing left of the town where Richard Hamilton lived those years after the Civil War. The only thing left is a marker where the courthouse used to be, the 'hanging tree', and the cemetery. On a visit there, my sister and I wandered around the cemetery awhile looking for any names we might recognize until we realized no one we knew would be in that cemetery. It was the 'white' cemetery. The Confederate flag on the gravestones should've been a clue that we were in the *Wrong Place*.

---

[7] The last words of this quote are illegible.

Fig. 4.2 We did manage to locate the infamous 'hanging tree' where it is rumored many a criminal swung. Pine Level, FL.

Still, as I sat on a gnarled tree half bobbing in the gently flowing Peace River and gazed through the brittle moss hanging from a nearby tree, I thought how much Arcadia looked like Williston.

Chapter 5

PICKINS WAS SLIM

Plural marriage was not uncommon in 19th century Florida. It wasn't exactly talked about, and it certainly was frowned upon by 'good' society. The Seminoles were very much a part of life for those scraping out a living in South Florida, and they too occasionally had more than one wife at a time. Traditional rules of marriage and divorce (among many other rules) were not of concern for the Indians, the freed slaves, and the general 'outcasts' of South Florida.

Florida slave narratives document that marriage between slaves was rarely a formal affair. Two people decided to be together and, with their master's permission, 'got married.' Divorcing was as simple as announcing that you were no longer 'married.' Formal marriage did not arrive until after Emancipation when missionaries and pastors roamed the country to encourage the former slaves to legalize their marriages. This mindset was probably not one that was forgotten quickly. While many former slaves happily legalized their marriages, there would have been some who preferred to hold to the 'ways' they had grown up with and practiced for over a century.

Life in Arcadia was rough. Richard was a former slave, a 'Negro' married to a white woman. Whatever his character was like as a child growing up in Springfield and Williston, antebellum Florida had to have taught him quickly how to fight. Later accounts of his character bear this assumption out. G. H. Watson states in a letter on October 7, 1902 that "one thing I will add that you have not asked for. When you have located your man, you will find a dishonest, contemptible, lawless vagabond and he a Negro having two living wives and families. None of which dare to live with him for fear of violence..."[1] It appears that quite a few people did not hold Richard in the highest regard.

We don't know what Richard Hamilton was like as a very young man, but we do know that he set out to build a large family within years after gaining his freedom from slavery. In his book *Man in the Everglades,* Charlton Tebeau states that Richard married in Pine Level and fathered four sons and one daughter. Richard makes no mention of this family in his deposition; in fact, he states that he never married. But marry he did.

> State of Florida. County of Manatee. To any regularly Ordained Minister of the Gospel, or Lawful Magistrate. Greeting - You are hereby authorized to join in the marriage relation Richard Hambleton (colored) and Hannah Moore and as soon as practicable after the performance of such ceremony, return this License to this office to be recorded. in wit___ whereof I have here unto ___ my hand and seal of office this Seventeenth day of April AD 1869. John F. Baitholf, Clerk Circuit Court, Manatee Co Fla.[2]

Richard and Hannah Moore had six children from 1868 to 1880. Walter Valentine, born October 1880, is listed under this

[1] Watson, G. H. Letter to J.A. Davis.
[2] Marriage License. Manatee Co. Florida. 1869

household and in the household of Richard's second wife, Mary Weeks. Hannah Moore's obituary states that she was the widow of Richard Hamilton, but there is no record of their divorcing. Likewise, the 1880 and 1885 census of Manatee County record that the spouse of Richard Hamilton was Hannah Moore.

In June 1880, Mary Weeks was living on one of the islands south of Punta Rassa. She was married to George Christian, who was 49 years old. Mary was 19.[3] Mary was unique in that she was one of a handful of people in the islands who had so many spellings of her name that sometimes it took some digging to determine if the information found was really about her. Most in the family from that time period remember her being called 'Apolony' most of the time. Other variants on her name include Abelona Christian, Mary Agnes Weeks, and Appollonia, Apolonia.

---

[3] Florida. Monroe County. Key West. 1880 U. S. Census.

Fig. 5.1 George Christian

After reviewing census records, the confusion that surrounds our Richard kicked into high gear. In 1885 Richard and Hannah lived in Pine Level with their seven children: Thomas, 18; William, 16; George, 12; Julia (called Jane in the 1880 census), 10; Benjamin L., 8; Walter, 4 and Robert, 2. Richard and all of the children were listed as mulatto, while Hannah was listed as white. Also living in the household, listed as a white housekeeper, was Apolonia (sic) Christian, age 22 and her daughter, Nina Hamilton, age 2 months and listed as white. Nina was listed in an earlier Arcadia census as the daughter of Mary Weeks and George Christian. Mary was listed in the household of Richard and Hannah on the census as a boarder.

We know that Apolonia Christian was also known as Mary Appolonia Weeks, the woman who settled in the Ten Thousand Islands with Richard in the early 1900's. Everglades residents later report that Richard "… is married and has a wife living with him. He is married to a "cracker woman, a white woman," says Joseph Pinckney. Nelson English of Key West says in 1896, "….It was reported (here) that he is married to a white woman and for that reason he cannot (live) here." Of which white woman is English speaking? By this time, Richard was living on and off with both Hannah and Mary in different cities.

In 1896, a minister named James Dean was interviewed because he was the sub agent for W. P. Canady during the Barrett pension investigation. He only knew Richard by the name Stephen Barrett. He told the examiner that Barrett lived on one of the keys near Chokoloskee. He recalled that a man was killed during this time period while being arrested by deputy sheriffs. The man had allegedly been charged with raping his own daughter. Dean says, "I rather think Barrett was in some way connected with that difficulty and had to leave the neighborhood." Dean also describes Barrett's wife as "a white woman or very nearly white."[4]

We don't know much about Hannah Moore. In 1920, She was living alone, as a boarder on Academy St. in Manatee County working as a 'celery hand in the celery fields.' She was listed as a 'widow,' although she was still married to the very much alive Richard.[5] In 1902, Richard tells a pension examiner, "I was never divorced from her. She never was divorced from me that I know of. I suppose she was living when I married Mary. Mary had been married before. His name was Geo. Christian. She left him and then married me. I could not tell you anything about whether they were divorced. He was living when I married her."[6]

Historian Canter Brown mentions in his book *Family Records of the African American Pioneers of Tampa and Hillsborough County* that Hannah died early on after the birth of her first son, Thomas. We now know that this is not true. She was very much alive when Richard gave his deposition in 1902. Her son George, signed her probate record in 1920.[7]

---

[4] Deposition A. James Dean.

[5] Florida. Manatee County. 1920 U. S. Census.

[6] Hamilton, Richard. Interviewed by JA Davis, Special Examiner.

[7] Probate Records. page 2122

In July 1859, Mary Appolonia Weeks proceeds to pop up here and there over the years, from Arcadia to Key West and points in between.

Mary is the daughter of Cape Sable pioneer John Weeks and Sarah Mercer. Sarah brought two daughters, Martha, born 1856, and Mary Elizabeth (Lizzy), born 1858, from her marriage to first husband, Jacob Raulerson. John Weeks would later tell William Allen Smith that Sarah was a "widdah."[8] However, further research shows that Jacob Raulerson actually did not die until June of 1886, so he was still living (and remarried) when Sarah Mercer and John Weeks married in 1858.

I found a marriage record listing Jacob and Sarah's marriage as 1855.[9] 1900 census records show that he was married to Mary Raulerson (maiden name unknown, possibly *Crew*) and they have two children, Martha and Lizzy living with them.

Regardless, some family records indicate that Appalonia[10] Mary Agnes Frances was born in 1863 and her sister, Sarah Jane was born in 1865 to Sarah Mercer Raulerson.

So, as was so common in those days of scanty recordkeeping and lost papers, we are left to wonder who Martha and Lizzy's mother actually was. Mary Raulerson or Sarah Mercer? The 1900 census also includes Liza Durrance, born 1864 and Sidney Durrance, born 1869 as children of Jacob Raulerson and Mary Raulerson. Cemetery records indicate that Mary Raulerson died in 1898.

In 1862, John Weeks and his third wife, Sarah Mercer Raulerson sailed down the west coast from Cedar Key and

---

[8] Copeland Papers: "History of the 10,000 Islands etc." 1927, p. 1085
http://www.naplesnative.com/CopelandPapers.htm
[9] Florida State Archive, Tallahassee and clerk of courts, various counties; Tallahassee, Florida; *Florida, County Marriages, 1823-1982*
[10] Spelled Appalonia on that document although many spell it Appolonia. I use the latter spelling throughout this book only because it was first presented to me that way.

settled at Chokoloskee Bay with Martha, Lizzy, and their baby daughter, Mary Appolonia. By John's account to William Smith Allen in the Copeland Papers[11], Sarah died there a few years later giving birth to Sarah Jane, called 'Sally' by the family.

Some years later, in 1878, when Mary Appolonia and Sally were older, John Weeks married his stepdaughter, Lizzy, and they had seven children: Matthew, David, Josephine, William, Alfred, John, and Mary Elizabeth.

This Weeks/Mercer/Raulerson connection is confusing. Faye Brown's book, *Weeks Family Connection*, is a great place to start. I've found myself spending considerable time pouring through other documents to verify information and will likely be doing so for some time to come.

Fig. 5.2 Sarah "Sally" Weeks

There are family accounts that follow the line of Sarah Mercer back to Moses Nunez who was involved in Indian trading in the late 1700s. It is said that he had possibly two Indian 'wives.' One of these was called 'Mulatto Rose' (she was part Indian and part black), and it is not clear if that is union from which Mary Appolonia descends. I have not found a birth certificate or any other document to corroborate the story.[12] Author of *Weeks Family Connection*, Faye Brown, says that our line descends through

---

[11] Copeland Papers: "History of the 10,000 Islands etc." 1927, p. 1085
http://www.naplesnative.com/CopelandPapers.htm
[12] Brown, Faye. *Weeks Family Connection*.

Moses Nunez and his first wife, Rebecca Abraham. Their son, Samuel married a woman named Mary Sharp and they had a son named Daniel. Daniel married Nancy (last name unknown). It has been suggested that Nancy was Seminole or Creek. The family was listed as Mulatto at this time.

Still, the discovery of Mary's lineage opens up the family line extending back six more generations, into North Carolina, England and Ireland (family names include Mercer, Embly, Hemphill), which is an incredibly exciting possibility for this genealogist.

G. H. Watson says in a letter to an unknown person, "____ Sir in reply _____ that a colored man known as Richard Hamilton also as Robert E Hamilton resides near here has been living since married the _____ one under the name of Richard Hamilton wife ____ ____ name _____ Robert Hamilton has been indicted for bigamy in Monroe Co Fla and claims to be Choctaw Indian descent. He first married a white woman; the wife he has now is mixed Blood." [13]This statement would point to Hannah Moore as the 'white woman' and Mary Appolonia as the wife with 'mixed blood.'

We don't know much about Mary Appolonia's first husband, Christian, either, other than that most records list his place of birth as Norway. In 1885, Mary had a daughter, Nina Hamilton, while residing in Pine Level. As Mary was living with Richard as a boarder at that time, it is unclear just who Nina's father was, or even if Mary was her mother. The child has Richard's last name. Christian was living next door, alone. Richard and Mary's son, Leon was also born on Fakahatchee Island in December 1885. So, either Mary got pregnant immediately with Leon after having Nina, or she was not the mother of one of them. And baby Eugene, who would grow up to be the family patriarch in the islands, is nowhere to be

---

[13] Watson, G. H. Letter to unknown. Everglade, Florida, 1902. Blank spaces were indecipherable words.

found at that time. He was born in 1883. Confused yet? Sometimes I feel as if I am juggling puzzle pieces.

So just who was Richard married to? Hannah Moore or Mary Weeks? Family legend says that Richard was a Mormon and had two wives and two families. Richard and Mary did marry, despite both of them still being married to others (Hannah Moore and George Christian respectively).

> I Certify, that the within named *Robert E Hamilton* and *Mary Weeks* were by me, the undersigned, duly united in the Holy Estate of Matrimony, by the authority of the within License. Done this 14th day of May A.D. 1890. Jose de Lamar Justice of the Peace.[14]

Which leads us to the family rumor that Eugene is not Richard's son at all.

Nellie, daughter of Eugene Hamilton, tells the story that Mary Appolonia (Nellie's mother in law) told her that a man named Daniels was actually the father of her son, Eugene (Gene). James Daniels, age 22 and wife Sarah, age 16, lived nearby to the Christians in 1880.[15] Recall that Mary and George Christian were married in 1880. She was living with Richard in 1885. They married in 1890. In 1900, James Daniels and his wife, Sarah, with their four children, lived next door to Richard and Mary in Chokoloskee. Daniels was listed as white and born in 1857. George Christian was also living there, again alone.[16] The story goes that when James Daniels was dying, he said he wanted to see his 'son,' Gene Hamilton. Family members confirm that Gene did travel to Chokoloskee to see the old man on his deathbed.

---

[14] Marriage License. Monroe Co. Florida. 1890
[15] Florida. Monroe County. Key West. 1880 U. S. Census.
[16] Florida. Monroe County. Chokoloskee. 1900 U. S. Census.

I suppose anything is possible at this point. I am reminded by a family member that "pickins' was slim in those days." A little bit southwest of the entrance to Chatham River lies Mormon Key. The story lives on to this day that Mormon Key was so named because of Richard Hamilton and his multiple wives.

Chapter 6

THE TEN THOUSAND ISLANDS

Map 6.1 Vignoles, Charles Blacker, and Henry Schenck Tanner. 1823

On an 1823 map, the Ten Thousand Islands has no name; it is labeled simply "Fertile Lands." To the southeast three words slash across the swamp: The Ever Glades.[1] For a short while, the Hamilton and Weeks clan lived in the Ten Thousand Islands, near Fakahatchee, Everglade and Chokoloskee. The names of these places have also changed over the years. In the late 1880s, Everglades City was called Everglade. It wasn't until the 1920s that the 's' was

---

[1] Vignoles, Charles Blacker, and Henry Schenck Tanner. Map of Florida.

added to the name by Barron Collier, forever renaming the entire area 'Everglades.' In 1952 the town of Everglades was officially renamed Everglades City. Fakahatchee was often called Fickahathee, Fakkahatchee, or Fahakahatchee, meaning 'Hard Bottom' in Seminole.[2] Chokoloskee also had variant spellings over the years, including Choucaluski Island. Later on, the Hamiltons would more or less settle for good in the Lostmans River region, south of Chokoloskee.

The Everglades was a good place to go for those attempting to find their way after reconstruction. The fish and game were plenty, and the land, that which was above water, was fertile. It was also the perfect place to hide for those running from the law. In 1885, one visitor wrote that "a man might hide himself here, providing he could only live and remain uncaught forever; tracking him would be impossible."[3] By 1898, Richard Hamilton was wanted by the government for pension fraud. He needed a safe place to raise his growing family. Given Richard's experiences in Manatee County, he must have been ready to disappear amongst the Indians and other people who just wanted to be left alone.

While the Hamilton family, especially Richard, are portrayed as 'desperados' and 'outlaws,' in reality they were mostly just trying to survive. They built stills and made moonshine, hunted egret for the plumes, killed alligators for the hides, turned sea turtles and sold the shells. They fought amongst themselves and outsiders. They did what they had to do to survive. They cultivated Indian middens and grew fruits and vegetables of all kinds. They migrated from island to island following the tides, fishing and crabbing and hunting along the way. They made charcoal and sold it. As the tourists and explorers began to arrive, they made money serving as guides.

---

[2] "Law's Technicality Frees a Murderer." pg 6
[3] "The Islands Off the Southern Coast of Florida." pg 2

The Ten Thousand Islands

In the early 1900s, the Ten Thousand Islands was fast becoming a popular tourist destination. Traveling by boat, their own or hired, these adventurers enjoyed fishing and hunting while marveling at the profusion of exotic plants and wildlife occupying each little spit of land. More than one visitor returned from a trip to the "Florida Islands" saying that the number of islands in the Ten Thousand Islands was closer to a million.[4] As more and more explorers and curious people undertook the arduous and exhilarating trip to the newly discovered Florida frontier, the local residents found themselves drifting farther down the coast in search of a quieter place to raise their families and fish, hunt, and farm in peace.

Richard, as well as most of the other locals, drifted around the islands between Everglade and Key West frequently. They had many different homesteads over the years, following the fish and occasionally being uprooted by storms and hurricanes. In 1880, Richard was the only mixed-race man on the Monroe county census listed as a farmer. The others listed as 'black' or 'mulatto' are listed as farm laborers. William Smith Allen is listed as living nearby. Allen settled in Everglade in 1870, taking it over after John Weeks (Mary Week's father) moved on. Weeks was known for wandering around; he rarely settled in one place for long. When Allen stopped at Everglade on his way to Key West and saw the amazing produce growing there, he determined to return later. He did and didn't leave until 1889 when he sold his properties to George Storter, Jr. for $800. Weeks and many others were employed from time to time by Allen as laborers on the produce and sugar farms. Weeks hauled sugar cane down to Key West on a barge.

So Richard and Mary Weeks settled down in the Ten Thousand Islands, and on the 1900 Monroe County Census they were listed as living with six children: Walter J., 18; Eugene

---

[4] "Saw a Million Florida Islands." pg 6

J., 16; John Leon, 14; Mary E., 11; Ann E., 7 and Mary, 4, all listed as black with the exception of Mary (known to the family as Appalony), who is listed as white. By this time, Nina had disappeared, and Walter, Gene, and Leon are all considered to be Richard's sons. In 1910, Mary was living on Summerland Key with two of her teenage daughters, an adopted son, Marion McCloud, and a hired man, William Bayley. She is listed as mulatto on this census, and Richard is nowhere to be found.

It wasn't just the tides that kept Richard on the move. He had made a reputation for himself during his time in Pine Level and trips to the islands. In 1899, Richard was arrested in Cape Sable for fighting with Frank Hamilton (no relation) and "Mr. Weeks. Richard apparently cut the two men very badly. A woman tried to help, and Richard hit her with a stick and told her he would cut her throat. The newspaper headline announced, "the notorious outlaw and Negro desperado…has at last been captured." The article does not describe the woman, other than that she is "old." Richard had previously told people, "No man living can arrest me."

Interestingly, the man who managed to arrest him was the infamous Edgar J. Watson, who had been made a Deputy Sheriff for a short time. This 'deputy sheriff' designation seems to have been used rather loosely. Watson found Richard on his boat and when Richard tried to get his gun from the cabin, Watson stopped him and arrested him. The local paper reported, "It is the opinion of everyone that Hamilton will go to the phosphate mines for his health. Cape Sable Sheriff Knight has certainly made a good and wise selection when he appointed Mr. Watson his deputy."[5] Many years later, according to family tales, Richard would be deputized long enough to arrest Watson. (See Chapter 12 Tall Tales)

Most accounts agree that Richard homesteaded Chatham Bend for a time before 'selling' it to Jean Chevelier, a

---

[5] "The notorious outlaw and negro desperado…"

Frenchman. Historian Tebeau notes that "Leon Hamilton and his sister Mary (not sure if he was talking about Mary Elizabeth or Mary Agnes) considered themselves godchilden of Chevelier."[6] Hamilton family stories corroborate that Chevelier was the godfather of some of Leon's children. Chevelier was noted for his interest in birds and plume hunting. Chevelier sold the homestead to Ed Watson around 1880. It is said that Richard decided that Chatham Bend was haunted by Native American spirits, so decided to move on to a less ghostly abode.

The family moved farther south and as the years passed, Richard and Mary raised their brood on a string of islands south of Chokoloskee and down to Lostmans River, which is located a bit north of Key West. Stories about how Lostmans got its name are as varied as the islands themselves. According to one source in 1927, "Lostman's River and (Lostman's) Key were named from the escapades of a party of deserting English. Sailors who were unable to escape from Key West by a fisherman who got their money and deserted them on the key telling them they would find a town on the other end of the island. They were found in a starving condition by Mr. W.S. Allen who took them to Punta Gorda."[7]

The family mainly lived around the area of Lostmans River after the 1910 hurricane drove them off Wood Key. Spellings differ. Lostman's. Lossmans. Lostmans. One newspaper calls the river 'Lawsonriver,' an interesting corruption of 'Lostmans River.'[8] In 1908, explorer A. W. Dimock writes, "At Onion Key-a Lossmans River landmark-we gathered and ate wild grapes and figs while coffee was being made for our luncheon."[9] This may not have been a corruption at all,

---

[6] Tebeau, Charlton W. *Man in the Everglades*, 93.

[7] "Saw a Million Florida Islands," 6

[8] Thomas, Fred. "Ah ha! Sleuthing News Hound on Local Sailors Trail," 6

[9] Dimock. "Crossing the Everglades in a Power Boat," Chapter 16, 219

however. In 1938, Surgeon General Thomas Lawson was put in charge of building a fort for the U.S. government on Cape Sable, just a short distance south of Lostmans River and Lostmans Key. There are some who believe the key and the river may have been originally named for Lawson. In 1920 Leon tells visitors to 'Lawsonriver' that tigers and panthers in the area have killed his "hogs, chickens and even got so hungry that they would kill his cats and dogs."[10]

Richard and Mary's three sons - Walter, Leon, and Eugene - were the children that never moved out of the islands until the bitter end. All three of these sons were born before Richard and Mary married. Richard moved around from Pine Level to Key West to Lostmans River. His women mostly stayed put, but one or the other occasionally turned up on a census with him. It wasn't until 1886 that Richard seemed to settle down finally in the Ten Thousand Islands, with Mary.

---

[10] Thomas, Fred. "Ah ha! Sleuthing News Hound on Local Sailors Trail,"
6

Chapter 7

WALTER JOSEPH VALENTINE HAMILTON

Fig. 7.1 Walter Joseph Valentine Hamilton

Walter Joseph Valentine Hamilton was born on October 31, 1880, in Pine Level, Florida. The genealogical debate has always been whether his mother was Hannah Moore or Mary Appolonia Weeks. In July 1880, Richard and Hannah lived somewhere in Monroe County with John Weeks, Adolphus Santini, James Daniels, and William Smith Allen living nearby. So, based on the list of inhabitants, that census was probably recorded in Key West or Chokoloskee. Mary Weeks is listed as Abelona Christian a short distance away, living with her husband, George. If Mary was Walter's mother, she would have been six months pregnant at the time of the census. Census records do not include unborn children, or anyone born before June 1880, so I think we can make a logical assumption here that Walter is Hannah's child, not Mary's.

In 1885, Walter was still living with Richard and Hannah in Key West, and Appolonia Christian is living with them. George Christian lived a little bit away, but still in Key West. Little Nina Hamilton is 2 months old and listed as white. No mention of her is found anywhere after 1885. In 1900, Walter lived in Richard and Mary's household. By then he was 18 years old and single, working as a fisherman.

By all accounts, Walter was a quiet man. Unlike his brothers, we don't find any newspaper accounts about him, no violence surrounding him, no incidents of trouble. Like all of the Hamilton family, he moved around frequently: Key West in 1885, Chokoloskee in 1900, Lostmans River in 1913, Hog Key in 1917, and Flamingo in 1920. In photos, Walter stands slightly slouched with his arms at his sides. His black hair had a bit of a curl to it and he wore a fairly full mustache in every photo. There is only one photo where he appears to feel confident, hands on his hips, staring directly into the camera. In that photo, his brother Gene and Charlie Tigertail stand near him. While he worked with his father and brothers from time to time, he kept mostly to himself.

Moonshining was a pastime that most men in the islands participated in, and apparently Walter was more serious about that work than most. He had several stills around the islands. I'm told that the remains of one of those stills is still out there on one of the islands, but we do keep some secrets in the family, so the person who told me that isn't talking.

Walter married three times, first to Minnie (last name unknown), with whom he had three daughters: Marie Violet, Annie Thelma, and Edna Cecelia. Then he married Lettie Pent, and they had one daughter. A year before Walter died, he married Alice Lenora Parker.

In 1893, the Dawes Commission set about dividing Indian lands into plots for specific tribes. Native Americans of the Five Civilized Tribes - Cherokee, Choctaw, Creek, Chickasaw, and Seminole - were required to apply to the Dawes Commission with their tribal affiliation. Walter and his wife Minnie both filled out applications - Walter as Cherokee and Minnie as Choctaw. Neither application ever came to anything because the Dawes Commission was overturned shortly after it was taken.

Fig. 7.2 Walter and Lettie Pent Hamilton. Lostmans River and Key West Florida.

Fig. 7.3 Walter J.V. Hamilton, his daughter Marie Violet Lovering, his granddaughter, Rita. 1940. Lostmans River, Everglades Florida.

Fig. 7.4 Walter Hamilton's place on Lostmans River

Fig. 7.5 Walter Hamilton's place on Lostmans River

Fig. 7.6 Walter Hamilton's place on Lostmans River

Fig. 7.7 1940. Lostmans River, Everglades, Florida. Walter Hamilton's home at Lostmans River. Alice Lowe, Walter Lovering, Walter J. V. Hamilton, Marie Violet Hamilton Lovering, and Baby Rita Lovering.

Fig. 7.8. Lostmans River, Everglades, Florida.

Chapter 8

EUGENE JOSEPH HAMILTON

Fig. 8.1 Eugene J. Hamilton (King Gene, age 18); Rebecca Johnson Hamilton (age 14); William J. Hamilton (age 2); Nellie Hamilton (age 6 months). 1906

Eugene Joseph Hamilton, called King Gene by most and Papa by the family, was born on October 9, 1883. He was born on the family boat, as were most children in those days, near Chokoloskee Island. It wasn't often that you would find a doctor out among the mangroves, so midwives would be called in when a birth was imminent. These midwives consisted of a handful of the local women around those parts. It is rumored by some that Richard Hamilton was known to step in as midwife on occasion. Many of the women chose the option of traveling to Key West or Fort Myers when the time came to give birth.

The family lived on their boat on Mormon Key mostly but traveled around frequently, following the tides and the fish. Mormon Key lies just a few miles south of Chatham River, a place that would become famous when the infamous Ed Watson moved there with his family.

In 1903, Gene married Rebecca, the daughter of Gilbert 'Gibb' Johnson and Emiline Holland. Gibb Johnson born in England, raised in the Bahamas, was a schooner master who sailed regularly on *The General George Washington* from Tarpon Springs to Key West. It was on this schooner that Gene and his brother, Leon met and married into the Johnson family. Gene to Rebecca and Leon to Rebecca's sister, Sarah. We see this quite often amongst the families there.

Gene and Rebecca lived on and around Turkey Key where they had nine children between 1904 and 1922: William (Buddy), Nellie, Ellen, Rosalie, Eugene (Josie), Ethel, Irene, Roy, and Eugene Mervin. Considering the mortality rate of children in those times, it is surprising that all nine of these children, with the exception of Buddy, lived long lives. I've read and heard many stories of children drowning out there in the islands. They were surrounded by water and most lived on boats, so this does not surprise me. They got around the waterways in lighters, small flat-bottomed boats with 'sweeps,' long oars.

In an interview, Uncle Genie (Eugene Mervin, youngest son of King Gene) says, "...my Aunt Sarah had a child by a former engagement or whatever that was born to her and at the age of two years old fell overboard at Turkey Key, 20 miles south of Everglades City and drowned at that time. Then she married Leon Hamilton and they had children." As far as I know though, none of Gene and Rebecca's brood were lost. Another story tells of how the 2-year old daughter of Gibb and Emiline fell overboard and drowned. Her mother found her the next day "resting at the bottom of the river."

Fig. 8.2 Lighter in the Smallwood Store Museum, 2018

Of these children, three would grow up to marry three of the Gomes clan. From that point on, the Hamilton and Gomes family consisted of a formidable family not to be reckoned with in Lostmans River. Buddy married Florinda Gomes. His sisters married Florinda's brothers. Nellie married Joaquin 'King' Gomes and Rosalie married Salvador Gomes. This made for some confusion down throughout the generations as we all struggled to untangle the brood of children that were Hamilton/Gomes.

King Gene's son, Eugene Joseph, (Josie as he was known to everyone around), was born deaf and never learned to speak. He was a genius though and was especially talented in boat building and working with engines. He once saw a houseboat that he liked and built it from memory. He put together many a boat from lumber he found washed up on the various shores of the islands. He was also known to rebuild motors from bits and pieces of broken wrecks.

Gene was not a large man in stature, but he was nonetheless a 'large' man. He commanded respect from his brood and got it. In every photograph I see of him, he is standing erect, strong legs spread out as if he is planting himself in the ground, daring anyone to shake him. In many photographs, his large hands rest solidly on each hip, and his gaze bores into the camera. You cannot help but feel the power behind the man. One descendent recalled being a pallbearer at Gene's funeral many years later. He says the casket was the heaviest one he had ever lifted. "I was one of the pall bearers. And that was the heaviest casket I ever remember picking up in my life. He wasn't fat, he was just stout. Solid. Not too tall."[1]

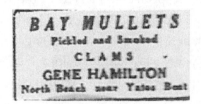

Fig. 8.3 Advertisement "Bay Mullets. Pickled and Smoked Clams. Gene Hamilton. North Beach near Yates Boat.

In his memoirs, my father, Ernest Hamilton writes, "My earliest remembrance of Papa is at Lostmans River. He homesteaded about ten acres right at the point. The place is now a Ranger station. His brother, Leon, lived right across the river. I remember Papa Gene standing, with legs apart, hands on hips, dressed in blue denim pants and shirt, on the porch of a wooden house built up off of the ground. I suppose he was surveying his flock and the lay of his land. We had to call him Papa. He lived over on Wood Key on occasion also.

---

[1] Gomes, Paul. Personal Interview, 2018

Eugene Joseph Hamilton

Paul Gomes, son of Rosalie Hamilton and Salvador Gomes recalls, "I remember he was a very strong man. I remember that up Wood Key there's a place called 'The Farm' where they used to grow all their produces and stuff. And I remember as a kid going up there, every year you'd have to go up and cut it out 'cause you couldn't get up this creek, cut it out to go up there. But Papa had everything in the world growing up there: figs, oranges, grapefruit, anything you could think of. It was an old Indian mound is what it was. He loved women, but so did the whole Hamilton crowd. He wasn't loud. All the people back in them days was pretty quiet. They didn't talk unless you talked to them."

Today, the National Park Service has renamed 'The Farm'. You'll find it on the maps now as 'Hamilton's Mound.'
While the family called him 'Papa' (still do), others in the area knew him as 'King Gene.' He was respected and feared by the inhabitants of the Islands. A deputy on Wood Key and personal friend of the Seminoles, he was said to possess a large tomahawk that he used on anyone who ventured into his territory. He was the favored guide for visitors and reporters, including Teddy Roosevelt.

Gene's youngest son, Eugene Mervin says,

"Now going back a little bit...my father...we knew the Indian chief. The Indian chief back then was named Charlie Tigertail. He was the only Indian chief that ever wore any clothes except the Indian tribe clothes. All the rest of 'em wore Indian skirts or whatever. I never saw an Indian those days that didn't come in an Indian skirt, the men. But Charlie Tigertail had dealt with Mr. Smallwood in Chokoloskee Island and he bought khaki pants, but he never was out of his Indian shirt. He had the pants but never without Indian shirt. And Charlie Tigertail was a man that knew the American people. He loved 'em, he knew his Indian tribe, he stayed with 'em. They had several of 'em,

Fig. 8.4 Charlie Tigertail, Walter Hamilton, King Gene

like Lucy Tiger, John Jumper, he was kinda hotheaded. They wanna fight, they wanna kill. Lucy Tiger killed the Indian chief, Charlie Tiger. They was a bunch of Tigers - John, Charlie., a whole bunch of 'em. They killed not Charlie, but John Tiger. His own cousin. And this come before the Indian counsel. They came and got my daddy to go and check on this here but they was all straightened out, everything was settled. They didn't have no Indian wars and everything was good with the Indian tribe."[2]

The issue of race continues to permeate this story, sliding its way in around corners and under doors every time I turn my back on it. It was not my purpose when I set out to discover my family history. But the more I dip into long hidden spaces, the more I find how much 'color' influenced everything. Indians and Negroes were not held in the highest regard by whites in this time. Richard, whatever his parentage, was clearly darker skinned than the average white man. His firstborn son with Mary Weeks, Walter, is the darkest of the family. Gene was lighter skinned. Leon had the lightest skin of all, and with his blondish hair, could pass as white. All of them are listed on the census records as black or mulatto until 1910 when they are finally listed as white. And that turns us back to parentage and blood lines.

On a visit to Chokoloskee in 2018, I spoke with a man who, upon learning my lineage, calmly said, "Oh, you mean the nigger Hamiltons."

I stared at him and let that sink in. He quickly attempted to apologize with something like, "Sorry about that, but that is what they called 'em back then."

I held up my hand to stop him, "Yep, that's me. That's my family."

---

[2] Hamilton, Eugene M. Audio recording. 1994.

He was familiar with the name Richard Hamilton and Walter Hamilton but not much else. I have a feeling he got most of his info from *Killing Mr. Watson*, as most people I meet tend to do.

Fig. 8.5 Gene Hamilton with wife, Rebecca and William Leo 'Son' Gomes (son of Joaquin 'King' Gomes and Nellie Hamilton). Circa 1941 Everglades

Chapter 9

JOHN LEON HAMILTON

Fig. 9.1 John Leon Hamilton

John Leon was born December 13, 1885 on Fakahatchee Island. When he was 19 years old, he married Sarah Elizabeth Johnson in Key West. They had four daughters and two sons: Mary Elizabeth, Eva Margaret, Robert Joseph, Adeline Agnes, Henry Gilbert, and Elizabeth Anne (Lizzie). All of the children were taught to read and write. Schooling, no matter how primitive or erratic, was important to the family, and all of the Hamiltons knew how to read and write.

Like his brothers, Leon was a fisherman. The Hamilton boys stayed close to Lostmans River: Wood Key, Mormon

Key, Turkey Key, Hog Key, Chatham Bend. They made occasional trips to Chokoloskee or Key West to buy and sell goods. He became known to the younger generation as 'Uncle Non.'

Leon had sandy blonde hair, made even blonder by the sun. He was a handsome man, as were all of the Hamilton boys. He had a medium build but was stout. Unlike his brothers, he had gray eyes rather than brown. Later in life, he was disfigured when he was attacked by an unknown assailant wielding a hatchet.

Gene and Leon had a falling out in later years. The story goes that old man Richard brought home a black family for dinner. Gene did not like this. Leon didn't like that Gene didn't like it. So, Gene and Leon parted ways. Leon moved further away, and Richard went with him and none of them ever spoke again. They saw each other now and then at family get-togethers and in business dealings. But the ties that bound were broken.

Fig. 9.2 Leon's place on Lostmans River

John Leon Hamilton

Paul Gomes recalls,

> "In the end, Papa and Uncle Non didn't talk. They all lived on Wood Key. And then the fight started and Uncle Non and Aunt Sarah and Grandpa Richard moved to South Lostmans. And for years and years they didn't talk. I don't think we did any visiting to speak of. In my time, we'd run into 'em every once in a while, somewhere, at the fishhouse or something like that. Every once in a while, we'd all go to Bonita Springs, that's where Papa moved after the park took over the land, and we'd have a big cookout and all of 'em played music. That was our immediate family, but Papa and Uncle Non never really got together, not while I was alive. The only time I know that they got together when I was alive was when Grandpa Richard died. Everybody went to Hog Key where we buried him, both sides, all the family. I was told he was 116. But I have no idea who told me or what come of it. I know he was old as hell. He was in his hundreds, I know that. I'm saying either '46 or '47, maybe even '45. Let's see, I was born in '37. That would have made me 8 years old. Anywhere between '45 and '48. Well, I know it wasn't '48 because that's when the park came and bought it all up and everybody had to leave. And everybody was still there when he died."

Matthiessen portrays this scene in his novel, *Bone by Bone* and writes that it is Henry Short, the black man who many insist fired the first shot that killed Ed Watson, who Richard brought to dinner. Henry Short was married to Richard's eldest daughter, Mary Elizabeth.

Fig. 9.3 Leon's place on Lostmans River

Fig. 9.4 Leon Hamilton

Fig. 9.5 Leon Hamilton and Sarah Johnson

Fig. 9.6 Leon Hamilton with some of the Hamilton children. Circa 1940

Fig. 9.7 Eva, Leon, Sarah Hamilton, unknown

Fig. 9.8 Gravesite of Leon Hamilton and Sarah Johnson. Fort Myers, Florida

Chapter 10

AMBUSH AT CHOKOLOSKEE

Fig. 10.1 Edgar J. Watson

Murder seemed to follow Edgar J. Watson wherever he went. He is reported to have killed the legendary Belle Starr and scores of others. Rumor has it that he killed off the workers he hired rather than pay them. After settling on Chatham Bend, a perfect hideaway for criminals on the run, Watson set about creating a plantation that became quite prosperous for that region. He had plenty of ideas for expansion and building his own little empire down in the Everglades, and many of the residents there did business with him regularly. Family stories tell how many a time Watson sat down to dinner with the Hamilton brothers. While not exactly friends with anyone, descendants of the Hamilton's report that their ancestors told them that Watson was a likeable man and friendly to most. Until late October in 1910.

Three of the locals, a man named A. Waller, another called Dutchy Reynolds, and a woman named Ellen Smith, were found floating dead in the swamp. One story claimed that they worked for Watson and he owed them a large sum of money. A black man, Sip Wilson, working with Watson told authorities that Watson ordered he and Leslie Cox, another wanted desperado who was often with Watson, to kill the three. Authorities searched for Cox but didn't find him. Watson maintained that he had nothing to do with the murders and he would personally find Cox and take care of him. One account says that he returned to the plantation, found Cox there, and killed him. He offered Cox's hat and coat as proof, but he refused to show anyone where Cox's body was buried. At that point, the people of Chokoloskee had had enough.

While the October hurricane of 1910 did much less damage than was expected, it still left the residents of the islands rattled and in need of replenishing their supplies. Everyone's nerves were on edge, from the storm and from the murders that followed in the storm's wake. On Wood Key, King Gene's clan was struck hard. The farm destroyed, supplies washed away, housing badly damaged, the family would be forced to move further south to Lostmans for a time. In the meantime, according to one family story, Gene Hamilton made his way north through storm debris to Chokoloskee to get supplies that were ruined in the hurricane.

Along the slow path littered with debris and rotting fish, Gene encountered Ed Watson who was on his way to Smallwood's Store to tell the men there that he had taken care of Cox. Gene told Watson that the men of the islands had had enough, and trouble was coming. Watson continued on his way anyway. Gene Hamilton watched events unfold from the shore, but according to him, he did not participate in the posse.

Gene's version of what happened that day are consistent with the version most told in the years to come. Watson pulled his gun, but it misfired, and the men opened fire.

Fig. 10.2 Ed Watson homestead (State Archives of Florida, Florida Memory)

Why did the men of Chokoloskee decide to kill their neighbor? Again, there are many suppositions, possible correct answers, but all we have to go on are tales from the eyewitnesses and newspaper accounts. Possible scenarios include: a) The residents were fed up with the violence in their community that seemed to always revolve around Watson and his cohorts; b) Watson was a known womanizer and there were too many of his illegitimate children running around already; c) The killing of Waller, Smith, and Dutchy was simply the last straw; d) all of the above.

Yet another paper reports that Watson and Cox both were killed on the shores of Smallwood's store that day. "E. J. Watson, a well-known farmer, and Leslie Cox, an escaped convict, under a life sentence for murder, were riddled with bullets last night by a posse out hunting the slayers of Miss Ellen Smith, A. Waller and "Dutchy" Reynolds..."[1]

Where was the rest of the Hamilton clan when Watson was gun downed in front of Smallwood's store? Richard's eldest

---

[1] "Murderers are Riddled: Two Men Who Committed a Triple Murder are Shot to death by Posse of Florida Men," 1

daughter, Mary married Henry Short in 1901. She was 13 years old. With the exception of Short and Gene, there were no Hamiltons near the shore that day that we know of. Again, the stories passed down through the generations can be taken as absolute eyewitness accounts or not. Already outcasts in a society of outcasts and adventurers, it is likely that the Hamilton family wanted no part of outright murder. The one black man that was present, Short, took the title of 'first shooter' for all the generations to come. As far as we know, the Hamiltons had no trouble with their neighbor, Ed Watson.

Fig. 10.3 Said to be Henry Short in front of Smallwood Store

Some are convinced that there was only one bullet that felled the fearsome Edgar J. Watson. They believe that the only shot fired was the one by Henry Short, who had been chosen by the residents of the area because he was such a good shot. The general consensus goes with the story that Short fired the first shot, and the rest followed suit. The story continues that Watson's body was later dug out of the water in order to count the bullet holes in his body, which by that time was impossible to do.

It is impossible to know who fired the first shot or who fired the kill shot, but local legend continues to place it on the shoulders of Henry Short. Perhaps the rest of the Hamilton family collectively decided there was no sense in getting white fingers pointing at them when the deed was done. Did they even know what was planned for that day? Rumors travel quickly in a small community, but the Hamiltons were not exactly part of the community. And word did not reach Watson either. He knew the air was unsettled, and he no doubt had his guard up, but did he realize that he was gliding his boat into an ambush? Also, the Hamiltons - Richard, Gene, Walter, Leon, and the rest were friends with Watson. Well, as friendly as was possible with a man like Watson. Perhaps they knew of the ambush and wanted no part of it for that reason.

The one eyewitness to what really happened at Chatham Bend days before Watson was gunned down disappeared. Sip Wilson, identified in almost every account of the Watson murder as simply "the Negro" or "the Nigger," was paid by authorities to leave town. So the story goes. Tales in the Ten Thousand Islands tend to shift and take strange turns depending on who is doing the telling. Sip Wilson ended up somewhere in South Carolina for the remainder of his days, no doubt trying hard to put the Florida Everglades far behind him.

As it is with most events of the past, and especially in those islands, we cannot know the true story. We create the possibilities, we mull over the many theories, and we each choose our own version of the truth. Or we simply accept that some things will just remain a mystery forever. Sometimes the mystery is more exciting than the truth.

After the showdown at Chokoloskee, Richard and his family, as well as the rest of the island residents, attempted to return to life as usual. As the census rolled around, Richard and his sons were occasionally listed as white on the census, a designation that meant nothing to the rest of the community.

The Hamilton family was destined to go down in history as 'the black Hamiltons.' This was not an issue for the majority of the clan, it just was the way the world was at that time. For Richard's son, Gene, though, this was just not acceptable, and he would spend his life trying to prove that he was as good as any white man in the islands.

As Richard approached 70 years old, he continued to move amongst the islands with his sons. On September 13, 1917 Mary Appolonia passed away at the age of 58 in Flamingo. It is said that she is buried under the Poinciana tree at Lostmans.

The Great Miami Hurricane made landfall the night of September 18, 1926. After tearing through Miami, the storm passed about 20 miles south of Fort Myers and then out into the Gulf. One news source reports, "The intensity of the storm and the wreckage that it left cannot adequately be described. The continuous roar of the wind; the terrifically driven rain that came in sheets as dense as fog...have left the memory of a fearful night in the minds of thousands that were in the storm area."

Back on Wood Key, Gene and Leon Hamilton, with their wives and a total of nine children, were marooned along with 23 other men, women, and children in the wake of the storm. After being rescued by the Coast Guard five days after the storm, they reported that they had lost their houses, their animals, their household goods, and all of their larger boats and had been sleeping on the beach and in a few small boats. By the time help arrived, they had resorted to chewing sugar cane and occasionally catching one of the few fish around for sustenance. The Coast Guard put up ten tents as temporary shelter for the families and left them with a supply of water and food to sustain them until more help could be sent.[2]

---

[2] Gray, Richard. Miami Weather Bureau Record, 412.

Chapter 11

TENDING THE TRIBE

The sons and daughters of Richard and Mary Appolonia knew no other way of life than the one they were born into on those islands. The white sandy beaches, oyster beds and coral reefs, mangroves and sawgrass, Spanish moss, and orchids was the only home they had ever known. Papa Richard taught them well. The Ten Thousand Islands was their hidden paradise, and for the majority of the years they lived and raised families there, the only access to their paradise was by sea. They knew their way around the islands as well as any Seminole guide. To come upon one of their homesteads in the mid-twentieth century was to encounter a scene that was anachronistic, a blast from some long past tribal abode. More often than not their humble lodgings consisted of a houseboat and several skiffs for fishing and navigating between islands. On the beach you would find all manner of animal skins being dried in the sun: alligator, panther, deer, rabbit.

On Gene Hamilton's homestead, one reporter detailed the shell mound where Gene had built his crude but functionable house. He describes the hanging baskets of fruit hanging in the trees and the profusion of trees - palms, live oaks, buttonwood, mahogany, and cypress dripping with Spanish moss and air plants.[1] Still, there were drawbacks to living in the islands, but the residents found ways to deal with them. One paper reports, "Swamp angels were an ever present annoyance during the

---

[1] Seabrook, William. "Paradise U.S.A." 1944.

warm season, but they carried mosquito bars wherever they went, built crackling fat-pine fires to ward off the molesters at night and dabbed kerosene on their skin during the day to discourage the insidious "no-see'ums".[2]

Changes were coming though. In 1922, the Tamiami Trail was complete and opened up the islands to even more tourists, explorers, and entrepreneurs.[3] Shortly thereafter the United States entered the Depression era. The Great Depression was a devastating period for many Americans. For roughly ten years, between 1929 and 1939, the country struggled to regain its footing in a shaky world. Banks failed. Savings were lost. Families watched as their homes were repossessed, and they took to the road, living vagabond existences. Children begged for food. Countless numbers of Americans died from illness and starvation.

The pioneers of the Everglades and their descendants however had little need for money and plenty to eat. Despite some inconveniences like mosquitos, alligators, and the occasional hurricane, the residents carried on with their lives as usual. They were surrounded by everything that they needed. My father, Ernest, told me, "I don't recall ever going hungry. The adults were strict, but us kids were happy."

I will let a few of the Richard's descendants describe what it was like growing up there, themselves having been born and raised there in the decades before the National Park Service took over.

The following memories and tales are from letters and interviews with several family members.

Eugene Mervin: From a transcription of an audio recording we found in my father's things. The speaker is Eugene Mervin

---

[2] Hawkins, Betty. "Santinis Plotted at Corse." News-Press, Fort Myers, Florida. 28 Mar 1970, 10.

[3] National Park Service. *Historic Roads.*

Hamilton, son of King Gene & Rebecca Hamilton. In our family, we called him Uncle Genie.

Junior: William Hamilton, eldest son of William 'Buddy' Hamilton, grandson of King Gene

Ernie: Ernest Hamilton, youngest son of William 'Buddy' Hamilton, grandson of King Gene

Paul: Son of Salvador Gomes and Rosalie Hamilton, grandson of King Gene

Shelter

<u>Ernie</u>

"The housing was pretty much the same anywhere you went. Unpainted boards, usually tongue and groove, maybe covered with black tar paper on the outside to keep the rain out and usually unfinished on the inside with 2 x 4s and single tongue and groove boards exposed. The inside may have partitions of wood or just simply material hung to provide separations. Until a permanent house could be constructed, folks lived in huts with palmetto tops (thatched roofs).

Fig. 11.1 unknown woman and man in doorway of stilt house

Windows were, for the most part, made of glass, but until glass could be brought in, people used some sort of treated cloth to cover the opening. Most places had screens in the doors and windows to stall the entrance of mosquitoes. The mosquitoes were always fierce, and sleep was facilitated by mosquito nets and by the burning of a smudge pot that produced smoke. It consisted of black mangrove charcoal and dirt. This material was placed inside the top of a coffee can or a bucket and ignited. The mosquitoes were still there when I visited in 1987. We used Crown Royal to fend them off!

Floors were most often made of wood with no covering at all. The kitchen floor may be covered with linoleum. There was no electricity. Lighting was accomplished with kerosene lamps, candles, or gas lanterns. Most times activity inside virtually stopped after sundown. Activities after dark usually occurred outside around an open fire. The big thrill were the ghost stories told around those fires.

All toilets were outside, usually some distance from the main house. At night chamber pots were used and emptied in the morning. The outhouses were also constructed with unpainted wood. The seat was made of flat boards with a hole or holes in it. Lime was periodically poured on the refuse to accelerate deterioration. Sears & Roebuck catalogs were available if someone had been to town recently. The pages were used for toilet paper. Many times, there was not even an outside privy. Living by the water provided a natural sewer.

We lived in many places, back in the 1930s and early '40s. One place we lived at several times, usually during the school periods, is in the center of my mind in memory. It was a little piece of high ground along the banks of the Caloosahatchee River, near the small settlement of Iona, Florida. We had a house, smoke house, small cabin, an artesian well, and of course, an outhouse, complete with Sears & Roebuck catalog. I believe in those years, fishermen were squatters, wherever they found an empty place they just moved right in.

Fig. 11.2 Hamilton and Gomes women and children

At another time we lived in a house built over the water near Turkey Key, still down in the Islands. One day while I was contentedly playing with my boats underneath the house, I was interrupted and forced to come topside to have my picture made. I was mad. I had to pose with Junior and Francis.[4] The picture hangs today in my office at home. It will give you an

---

[4] Junior and Francis were Ernest's older brothers (all sons of William 'Buddy' Hamilton and Florinda Gomes).

idea of what the houses looked like. I'm glad they forced me. I look at that picture on occasion and pause to remember the good old days. In 2002, I took pictures of the remains of that old house – black, rotted poles jutting out of the water, far out from the island it had once been near – the product of time, hurricanes and erosion.

Fig. 11.3 Buddy's three boys: Ernest Eugene Hamilton, William Joseph Hamilton, Jr. Francis Salvador Theodore Hamilton, circa 1935

Down in the Ten Thousand Islands we lived for a while on a lighter. A sort of houseboat, except this one also had a fish house on it. Bill Parker, my stepfather, tended the fish house. He would dock up at various places from time to time, and the fishermen would come to him with their catch. Once he had a decent load, he'd head for the main fish house at Chokoloskee or Everglades City."

Fig. 11.4 Unidentified woman on one of the keys in the Ten Thousand Islands

Junior

"My people were fishermen. We traveled and moved to many different places. Wherever the fish were running, we went. We lived in a lot of unpainted shacks and tarpaper sided house or lived right in the boat.

One of the places we lived in the late 1930s was Mormon Key. At Mormon Key there were five houses built over cisterns. Four were in a single line near the beach and the one we lived in was sitting on the top of one of the Indian mounds, sitting back about 150 feet from the beach. In other words, pretty close to the middle of the Key."

Paul

"Probably fifty percent of the housing was lighters. And the other was shacks and stuff on different islands, everybody picked a different part of the island."

11.5 Remains of Gene Hamilton's cisterns on Wood Key

Fig. 11.6 Remains of Gene Hamilton's cisterns on Wood Key

Fig. 11.7 Ernest E. Hamilton, Jr. examining the remains of his great-grandfather's cistern on Wood Key.

Food

<u>Ernie</u>

"There was curlew to knock out of the trees and which made the best 'chicken' and rice. There were the turtles to turn and the eggs to find and boil. We would walk the beach with Mama and stab the sand with a long stick until we found the turtle eggs. One time we were camping on an island where we had located turtle eggs. We found a bunch one particular day and boiled all of them, or so I thought. We boys were having a lot of fun. Running, swimming and eating boiled turtle eggs.

The eggs very closely resemble ping pong balls. The insides, after boiling, look and taste like the yolk of a chicken egg. We had eaten a lot of eggs that day but still wanted more. The adults first said there were no more, then somehow found two more. Francis and I both grabbed them, and in the usual manner, broke open the skin with our teeth and sucked the egg dry. We heard a lot of laughing from the others.

"What's so funny?" we asked.

After they were able to stop laughing, they explained that those two eggs had not been cooked. Some joke! We gagged and ran down to the water, frantically trying to wash the taste out of our mouths with sea water. It was god-awful!

There were wild hogs to hunt and boil for the lard. There were oysters, clams and all manner of shellfish to cook or simply eat raw. There was all the fish anyone would ever want, mostly always fried in hog lard, together with grits.

There were coco plums, sea grapes and a large variety of wild berries and fruit to pick and eat or jar.

There were homemade biscuits, the corn dodgers (fried cornbread), johnnie cake (fried flour dough) and light bread on occasion, whenever they made it into town and there were the homegrown fruits and vegetables and all the jarred jellies and jams.

There was always a pot of lima beans on the stove, starter dough in the flour barrel and always lots and lots of seafood. The stove was wood. They had a pretty good life without a lot of money."

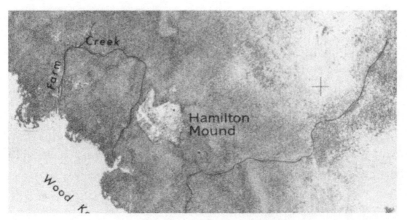

Map 11.1 Hamilton Mound

This map shows *Hamilton Mound*, so named by the NPS (National Park Service). Residents there simply called it *The Farm* before the park took over. King Gene grew a profusion of vegetables there. To the south is Lostmans Key where the Ranger Station was located. Gene owned this Key for a time. His brothers, Walter and Leon lived nearby.

<u>Junior</u>

"Close to where we lived there were a lot of guava trees and us three boys - me, Francis and Ernest - really loved the fruit. They were big and juicy and had hundreds of seeds in them. We would eat a bunch of them every day and you guessed it...we would get constipated and Mama would use her home remedy on us. She would sit each of us on the potty and then tell us ghost stories."

Fig. 11.8 Unidentified man and women

Fig. 11.9 Back of photo reads "Taken April 1 1928 Losman's River Fla."

I went to visit my father, Ernest Hamilton, to get him to tell me the names of some of the people in photographs. I found one picture of a skiff with a big alligator next to it. That sparked him off. He told me about how Bill Parker (his stepfather) used to take him out on the skiff when he was about 7 years old. Parker would make him dangle a baby alligator over the water. The baby alligator would scream and scream for his mama. And when the mama surfaced to get her baby, Bill Parker would shoot it between the eyes. I asked what they did with the baby alligator after that. Daddy says he imagines that they kept it for a little while to use again and he can't recall what they did with it after that. He says they used to have alligator skins nailed up on the side of the house all the time. Then they would sell the skins, of course.

Daddy shrugs, "Just another way of making a living." Then he grins and says, "I guess this was how they afforded to live on the waterfront."

Paul

"Everybody had plenty to eat. That was my job in the evening, to go take the skiff and go down on the port - that's a little island - and certain islands the curlew flew over. My job was to shoot the curlew, and I always had to shoot the brown ones because they were young. That's how I became a pretty good shotgun shot.

We cooked on a gas stove, about 24-inch, four burner, had a little oven. My mother was a good cook. About all those people were good cooks. They had to be. I make a mean johnny cake. No recipe; you just gotta practice. It's just flour, water, and salt. Mix it up, make a little ball, put it in the pan, and squash it down, flatten it. Lot of grease. Back in them days it was a lot of lard. They talk about this stuff, but you know, a lot of those people lived to be old old people, smoking all their life, eating lard.

The ice we got was from the fish house, came down with the runboats.

115

There was hardly any trash. Your bread was baked. You had some canned goods. They probably threw those in the water cause they were all made out of steel, iron, tin, they probably would be dissolved by the salt water in 6 months. We didn't have no plastic and all that stuff."

Ernie

"Out in front of our place, way out in the river close to the channel marker, was a huge oyster bed. We went out there to gather oysters. We'd take knives and vinegar and eat our fill of raw oysters before we headed home to have a heaping plate of fried oysters for dinner. Back then we called it supper, can't remember when the name changed. We had lots to eat, as I recall. A farm was nearby. I don't know the arrangements Bill had with the farmer, but we had every kind of vegetable imaginable. Although the country hadn't completely emerged from the Great Depression, times were good as I remember. Seafood of all kinds; alligator, fish, shellfish; wild meats; hog, deer, curlew; vegetables; okra, squash, beans, potatoes, Irish and sweet potatoes, cabbage, carrots, and on and on. Of course, we went into town on occasion and also got some store-bought stuff."

Getting Around

Ernie

"The cars in those days, at least in our neck of the woods, were of the 1928-32 vintage. They had to be cranked from outside in the front. It was not uncommon to see cars parked on the side of the road with the driver repairing a flat tire. Everyone carried a boot to plug up large holes in the rubber. A boot was another small piece of rubber that fit inside the tire and could cover a large area of worn-out tire. It gave you more mileage for your tires. Everyone also carried inner tube patching material, rubber patches, glue and a scraper to clean the tube where the patch was to be applied, a hand pump and a jack."

Cars in Everglades City, 193? (Florida Memory.com)[5]

Fig. 11.10 Floating Fish House

Getting the fish that they caught to actual market was not always an easy task. The trip to Key West from Lostmans River was long and many fishermen didn't have a boat with a motor.

---

[5] *Cars parked near the Collier Corporation Administration Building in Everglades City.* State Archives of Florida, Florida Memory.

Fig. 11.11 Floating Fish House

So, the floating fish house was towed around to various island locations so fishermen could sell their catches.

Paul

"Most everything we ate, we caught or killed, so it was fresh. We had runboats, running from Everglades and Punta Gorda down to the fishhouses on Lostmans River and around there. A fish house was a big lighter and they had a room with ice to keep the fish and stuff. We could send a list with a runboat and next time they come down there, they brought it down. And that's how you got your canned goods and stuff, flour, sugar, coffee.

Riggs Fish Company, was the main fish house in Everglades. It was a company store, same like with the coal miners. You didn't even have to pay for it. They'd send the goods to the fish house, and they would deduct it from money you got every week."

Making a Living

<u>Junior</u>

"Our main livelihood was fishing, we fished along the river (gill nets) for mullet, and a lot of different kind of fish, we always threw the catfish back in the water, there was no market for catfish then. When we weren't fishing, we were hunting gators and coons, and when I say we, I mean Bill Parker, my stepdad, and myself.

It's better to hunt gators and coons at night. We had a battery light mounted on a carbide light cap, powered by a 6-volt car battery. We would paddle the river and creeks looking for them and once you spotted their eyes in your light, (it had them blinded as long as you had their eyes in your light), we shot the gators with a 22 rifle. So as not to mess up their hide we'd shoot him between the eyes, it stunned him for a few minutes, then you'd grab him by his mouth and hold his jaws together. Next, you use a long-bladed hunting knife or hatchet and stick it in him right behind his eyes in the center of his back and break his backbone where he couldn't move around and harm you. Next morning you would skin him, rock salt his hide, roll it up and stow it. A coon you would shoot in the head if possible, skin him, and tack his hide on a square frame to dry.

Our skiff that we fished and hunted in was made out of cypress lumber, it made it light where you could pick it up by hand and lift or carry it with not much of a problem."

<u>Eugene Mervin</u>

"I'm Eugene Mervin Hamilton, the son of Rebecca and Eugene Joseph Hamilton. I was born 1923, May the 4th in Key West, Florida on Catherine Street. My mother said I was born about 8:20 in the morning. And mean as you know what. But anyhow, as I grew up in Key West as a young boy, I saw the changes made and as my father worked...my family...we went from Key West to Everglades City and a place called Lostmans River where my dad had the fish camp and where they were building this road, I believe I said earlier from Poinciana to Ochopee. My dad had a place, at that time he owned it and as I said...had about 100 to 150 blacks cutting the mango trees down. But I lived there and every season I went back to Key West to go to school. Well, I went from there to the grammar school, the St. Joseph's school on Simonton St. in Key West.

As I went there, just being a Catholic, I was born and raised a Catholic and my family's all Catholic. I was raised there, and I went to school there. And it's going there I became confirmed, and baptized at the age of 12, in the Catholic church there on Division St., in Key West, Florida. From there I studied to be an altar boy at the age of 12. I was an altar boy under the priest, which is Father Daughtry and Father Moory,[6] for four and a half years. And I said that was a hard study, but good. I went on to finish 11th grade in the Catholic school in Key West on Simonton St.

From there, as a young man, I worked...I grew up in the grocery store business with my father. I worked in the grocery store business, and I got my own fish market at the age of 16 in Key West, Florida. I also worked in a pineapple factory for Lamar Thompson in Key West. I saved all the pits and bits whatever that you can get and I sold them. I even made pineapple wine and gave it away.

I had fun back those days as a young boy growing up. I used to ride into Garrison Bight where my dad kept his boat up there. If you ever go to Key West, you'll find that Garrison Bight has an overpass now that goes from Truman Blvd to downtown Key West. There, as I grew up as a boy, I used to go out at nighttime and catch crawfish and sell 'em. Sold 'em

---

[6] Both of these names were transcribed from the audio recording, so the spelling may not be accurate.

for 10 cents apiece. And then was glad to get my money from people. Cuz they didn't have any money back in those days.

As I grew up in Key West, we had cigar factories, we had pineapple factories, we had turtle kraals, we had just about anything a young man wanted back those days. We didn't have pot. We didn't have marijuana, or rock or whatever back those days. We'd just drink my pineapple wine and had a good time. That's about the way it stood me and I'm proud of my family."

<u>Junior</u>

"Now living far inland, I think about sitting on a strip of white sand and looking at the ocean, watching the white seagulls and the sun going down behind the sea. I see with misty eyes the vision and memories of the Ten Thousand Islands in the 1930s, the people and families that lived there, Hamilton, Gomes, Padilla, Parker, etc. Coon and gator hunters, clam diggers and, I suppose, desperadoes.

We lived in an ole abandoned fish house on the east point of Turkey Key. We had net spreads along the side of the house. It seemed that we always fished at night. We would boat our net and as the twilight blue that held and deepened toward darkness, we moved out and met with other fisherman and made many strikes. A strike is when you put your net down in the water, usually in a circle.

In all the world there was only a small vagrant breath of restless night wind, and we would find a clearing and make camp. Then we would build a small fire and have a fire-blackened gallon can of coffee with cold biscuits and fresh fried mullet. After the meal, the men would get out their Bull Burham tobacco and smoke their pipes or brown paper cigarettes."

Tending the Tribe

Eugene Mervin

"They farmed. They grew cane. They grew corn. They grew potatoes. And they cut cordwood, black button wood or cordwood to survive in those days. And they traded with old man Ted Smallwood of Chokoloskee Island, several other guys in Everglades City. Plus, the Indians. My dad and my grandfather had traded with the Indians for years.

As my daddy grew older and moved from Mormon Key and married my mother, he moved to Lostmans River, which he owned, Lostmans River and Wood Key also.

And then my dad opened a grocery store as a young man at Lostmans River and then he started trading with the Indians, I said before. And the Indian trade...I had seen the Indian tribe come to our place at Lostmans River and looking back over the years, they would bring their families down, after they got to know my daddy.

He was a Deputy Sheriff at Monroe County at that time. And they always called him when he was real busy, and he want to say something, they'd say 'huckle-me-hine-ere.' That meant he was a high sheriff of Monroe County. And then when they want to get arrested, they'd say 'huckle-me-hine-ere' and my daddy'd put handcuffs on 'em to show them that he could take 'em to Key West. This was all in play, fun, and no real bad things, because they always respected my daddy.

But looking back, seeing 'em...they brought their wives, their squaws, their children. I used to wrastle with the boys, used to play with the girls. Out open, just have a good time. That's right. Had a good time with 'em.

This is the way I grew up at Lostmans River with my dad and my family. My dad was a wonderful person. He knew everybody. He could speak the Indian language. And everyone respected him as far as the Indians were concerned."

Fig. 11.12 Unidentified men

Junior

"We had an ole 1928-29 dark gray four door Overland sedan with red pinstripes.

In the afternoon we put our 12-foot skiff on top of the car. We moved up our shell road and then went along the Tamiami Trail until we came to Tanner Creek. There we floated our skiff and as the sunset sky cooled into grayness and the evening stars began a first faint winking, a chill wind with a smell of frost in it would drift through the mangrove swamps.

There we started our hunt for gators and coons. The first gator Bill spotted, he shot it. They don't float, you have to grab them right away and Bill missed him, and he sank. We searched the small area for it, and finally spotted a stretch of white lying on the bottom of the creek. "Gators have a white belly," Bill said, "There he is, Junior, slip off your shirt and breeches and go down there and grab him by his mouth and bring him up. I'll keep the light on him for you."

I got in the water and went down and when I got the white object it wasn't the gator; it was a white pillowcase. I came back up with the pillowcase in hand and surprised Bill as much as it did me. He reached down and jerked me up into the skiff; we were real nervous, upset and excited at this time. That finished us for that night. We loaded our skiff on the car and went home. To this day, I still wonder if that ole gator lived on into an old age and never was made into a handbag or shoes."

In 1920, Leon regaled some tourists with stories of tigers and panthers running wild and killing his hogs and chickens. He told them the wild animals even kill his dogs and cats. This was a regular activity at the time. People came from all over to experience the beauty of the Everglades. Many, many times they left vowing to never return.

The Hamilton clan, along with other families, served as guides to these tourists on a regular basis. It was a good extra income to supplement their fishing and trapping activities.

Medical

Ernie

"There was a big abandoned fish-house icebox on the grounds in front of the house a little to the northwest. Just next to it was a very large seagrape tree. We played there a lot.

One day Francis and I were playing in and around the icebox in the yard. Francis jumped off, tumbled, and stepped on a broken bottle, which pierced the top of his foot making a big gash and causing the blood to spurt. He yelled, of course, and Mama came running. She took in the situation with one sweep of her eyes and ran for the house. She reached up into the eaves of the roof and gathered a handful of cobwebs and ran back to Francis. She applied the cobwebs to the wound and kept it pressed there. It was an effective coagulant. The bleeding stopped. She then piled him and me into the car, a model A Ford, and drove to the doctor's office in Fort Myers, about ten miles away. He probably got a beating for it, but I don't remember.

The main store-bought medicine kept around the house back then was Black Salve. It came in a can similar to shoe polish. It was applied to most ailments and sores. Of course, Castor Oil was always handy and was used to cure most everything. You couldn't take it straight. It had to be mixed with orange juice or something.

We always seemed to have boils – also called risens. I'm guessing they were born of uncleanliness. We probably didn't bathe all that often. These things would swell up on one's arm or leg, get red and tight, and eventually form a head. When that happened Mama would apply a poultice made from cactus. She would go into the woods, cut a cactus leaf from the plant, pull or cut the stickers out and cut it into slices which would be used to cover the boil. In short order the boil would have erupted and begun to diminish in size and pain."

Junior

"One day a group of us went out fishing (gill netting) for mullet. We had a 22-foot motor launch and three skiffs. In the group there was me, Bill and Robert Parker, Montville Hamilton, Uncle Walter Padilla and his son Ray. We left our place and started searching the river and finally Bill spotted a lot of mullet flipping and said, "We'll make a strike here." We did, using three nets in a big circle, and then we moved our skiffs to the middle of the circle and stomped on our boat seats and banged our poles and oars against the side of the boat to scare the fish into the net.

It was decided we would work the nets into a tighter circle and cast net the rest of the fish out. In order to work the nets in you have to get in the water, using your feet to pull the lead line to keep it on the bottom. Then you use your hands to pull the cork line and bunting. At this time Bill and Monty took one side and Uncle Walter and Robert took the other side and they started making the circle smaller. Ray and me took care of the skiffs, anchoring them away from the nets.

As they were working the nets, Robert got to splashing in the water and hollering, "I've been stuck, I've been stuck!" Everyone quit what they were doing and went to Robert's aid. We got him into the skiff, and you could tell by the way he acted and his moaning that he was in pain. We took him over to the launch and put him aboard it. Someone said, "It looks like he's been struck in the foot by a stingray. Might be broke off in there."

Blood was gushing out of his foot. Bill took an old shirt and twisted it together and made a tourniquet of it. He wrapped it around Robert's leg using a screwdriver to tighten it up to stop the blood. Uncle Walter said, "I'll use one of my remedies to ease his pain." He got a bucket and filled it half full of gasoline and put Robert's foot in it. After a while Uncle Walter asked Robert if it felt any better. Robert said it was real cool and the pain seemed to be going away.

Bill took Robert on into Fort Myers to see the doctor and the rest of us stayed there to retrieve the nets and fish. Robert recovered nicely later on."

Ernie

"In 1937, Bill Parker ran a fish house at Fort Myers Beach. We lived in an old house near the fish house at the edge of the water. I was playing in the big open area when Mama yelled out the door, "Ernest, you're five today." I was very happy and ran into the house for a glass of orange juice.

Another day while I was still five, I was playing outside when Junior came over to where I was with an ice shaver, a big saw-like tool on the end of a handle used for shaving huge ice cakes. Junior was ten.

He said, "Put your foot out and let's see how close I can come."

I did, like a dummy. He jabbed the shaver towards my toe and missed it by a mile. This was fun! He tried again. This time

126

he got too close. He split my big toe in half. I screamed. Mama came out and took me in the house and gave me orange juice. She gave Junior a good whipping.

Another day while I was running around out there, I jammed a nail into the bottom of my foot and received my first lesson in how to avoid lockjaw. Tetanus shots do the job today. That day, I beat the bottom of my foot with a board until it bled. Blood, and poison, ran out onto the ground. I did not get lockjaw. I doubt if a doctor, assuming there was one around someplace, could have done any better."

Chores & Child Rearing

Ernie

Fig. 11.13 Rosalie and Nellie Hamilton. Both married into the Gomes family.

"Mama (Florinda Gomes Hamilton) would carry buckets of freshly made syrup from the refinery to the assembly building where the syrup was canned and made ready for market. She worked on the farm to help with the harvest of all sorts of vegetables and fruit, including bananas and avocados. She, of course, also participated in the cooking and tending to the young'uns.

My mama did her share around the place. She boiled clothes in a big black pot, jabbing at them with a stick to keep them stirred. She chipped an Octagon soap bar into the brew until the suds were foaming. After a while she would pick the clothes out of the pot with the same stick and throw the clothing over a clothesline. After the clothes were cooled off a bit, she would wring them out and hang them proper on the line. Once they were dry, she'd fold them and put them away. This chore, on more than one occasion, included the clothes of others in the clan.

Fig.11.14 Rebecca Johnson Hamilton with the children

Our folks wanted their shirts and pants ironed when they went into town. The tool of choice was a piece of iron shaped like a boat and flat on the bottom with a handle on top. It would be placed on the stove to heat and then picked up using a rag to grasp the handle and then applied to the garment. Needless to say, if the iron was not constantly in motion, the material would sport a brand-new hole to be patched.

Bill (Parker) also dispensed gas to the fishermen. One day my brother, Francis, found the gas hose and sucked on it. He passed out and Mama thought he was dead. He revived only to get his rear-end whacked good and proper and admonished to keep his paws, and mouth, off things not concerning him.

Wallopings in those days were the order of the day. Children then as today took their chances and did some things they were not supposed to do. When they got caught, they knew what to expect. Another rule for children then was, and I heard it many a time, 'children are to seen and not heard'."

<u>Paul</u>

"Water for bathing, cooking, and laundry. About once a week you had a #3 washtub, all the kids go in the washtub, you use the same water cause water was like gold. A lot of people, including my mother, took what we called a 'whore's bath' you know, underneath the arms."

Schooling

<u>Paul</u>

"My daddy was a fisherman, and what you did as a fisherman, you followed the fish. Different seasons there's different fishes and they'd move up and down the coast. So, in the wintertime, a lot of times, we'd go to Marathon. I went to school in Marathon, in the Susan B. Moore school. They've got a big statue of her, what a bitch. She failed me two grades in a row, and when we finally left there and moved back to the

Everglades, the teacher said, "This is sinful. What are you doing in my class?"

She moved me up to the 2nd grade, then she moved me to the 3rd grade, then she moved me up to the 4th grade. She says, "I don't know what that woman was thinking about."

I said, "I do! The bitch didn't like me."

So anyway, the fish, we moved up and down the coast. We'd go down in the winter, winter in Marathon. Daddy'd fish out of there. Then the summer, we'd come back and fish all of Lostmans River, and then when school started, Daddy'd go up to Everglades, and I'd go to school, me and my brother and sister would go to school. And then, soon as we got out of school, like for Christmas or whatever, we'd go back to Lostmans River. Like nomads, right? It was an interesting life. We would get books from the Catholic church in Key West, and I'd study those. Until we started going to school in the Everglades, on the lighter."

Ernie

"I began school at the Iona school on McGregor Boulevard. The school is about two miles, more or less, from our house in a southerly direction. It is a small brick building and looked then quite like it does today. Our route to the school, and I believe we walked it, began on our old dirt or shell rock road, across the farm, across the first paved road, continuing south until we reached McGregor, then west to the school. The school contained two, rather large, classrooms. One for high school students and the other for all the rest. In the middle of the room was a potbellied stove, which used wood for fuel. In the winter it always held a pot of boiling water, to provide humidity, I reckon.

One day they had some sort of festival. All the young ladies in high school baked pies, which were to be auctioned. The young high school boys were supposed to be the bidders.

Junior liked one little gal pretty particular, and he bid a whole dollar for her pie. I believe he won. I don't know where he got such a sum to pay off. If Bill had to pay, I'm sure Junior got a licking for it.

There was one time, shortly after I had begun school, when we had homework. We were supposed to study a list of words for a spelling test the next day. I thought we were supposed to memorize them. I did, and when the teacher told us to prepare to take the test, I wrote them all down. She was amazed. I spelled them all correctly too. I always was a good speller. That is my only visible and known talent."

Chapter 12

TALL TALES

Dear Karen,

I received your letter, was real happy to hear from you, and thanks for liking my little stories, but it probably won't make too good a book. It is a good idea to save all this stuff. Take, for example, your own family. How much do you know of who they were, how they lived, and how they thought three or four generations ago? Like me, I usually know something about our grandparents and maybe a little about great-grandparents, but past that, all that remains are names, dates, and maybe a few places.

Unless something has been wrote down, like in the Bible, Napoleon, MacArthur, Patton, etc., and diaries, nothing is remembered too good and all our past is like a cloudy dream with a few rays of light, old tax or military records, land transfers and the like, and after this we have nothing of who these people were. I do believe that now that Mama and most all the rest are gone, I suppose it would be good for me and Hank[1] to write down all that we remember, for all the ones behind us. At least they would have a little something to go on.

---

[1] Referring to his brother, Ernest.

I don't remember too much about Dad. But Mama was a real trooper, trying to raise three kids back in them days. And we had a stepdad for a while, William David Parker. In '32, when Dad disappeared, I remember very little, but I've heard lots of hearsay. I'll come up with what I remember in the future, ok?

Take care and God bless you and yours,

Love, Boats (Uncle Bill)[2]

The Bone Pile

At its core, the Hamilton family was like any other. I imagine that they sat around the campfire at night, watching the flickering sparks float overhead and light up the dark sky on a half-moon night. They drank and 'shot the breeze,' as my daddy would say. There was no television made up stories to distract them from the far better reaches of their imaginations. I have had the pleasure of sitting at my father's feet listening to him and his brothers laugh and tell stories, some true, some embellished to the point where fact floated off with the fire's embers and joined the stars. After a while, it just stops mattering where fact ends, and imagination takes hold.

One such story is the story of the bone pile. The reality is that these people lived on an island. They hunted and killed and ate what they could find. With that occupation comes the parts of the animal that are of no use, at least not immediate use. The skulls and femurs, tibias and spines, the bones of deer, alligators, and panthers were the real source of the infamous bone pile. In one article, the reporter laments that King Gene wouldn't let him photograph the bone pile.

I imagine Gene found this amusing, saying in his fiercest voice, "No. I can't allow you to take pictures of that." Sinister

---

[2] Hamilton, William J. Letters to Karen Y. Hamilton, 1990.

like. He had a reputation to uphold after all. And I can see the lot of them sitting around the campfire or floating along the back alleyways of the swamp and just laughing heartily at this tall tale. The trash pile of leftover bones turned into something sinister and mysterious made for an excellent family legend, as well as protection from outsiders.

The Tomahawk

There is a story that supposedly started the legend of King Gene's tomahawk. The story begins with a man on the run from some alleged violent act he committed in New England. We, of course, know that Gene was born and raised in the Ten Thousand Islands; he never stepped foot in New England. Well, that we know of anyway. The tale says that this 'Gene Hamilton' kept company with Alpheus Kirby, and the two of them hunted and fished all along Lostmans River. A Seminole occasionally joined them, and they used dugouts to trap and fish up and down and around the little islands. All was well.

Fig. 12.1 Rebecca Hamilton, King Gene Hamilton, and Butterball Knowles. Photographed for an article written by William Seabrook in 1944

Sometime later, a beautiful Indian princess laid her soft doe-like eyes on Kirby and fell in love. They married. In the course of time, two children were born. Again, all was well on Lostmans River. Until one day, the Seminole princess realized that she was in love with the handsome, tall, and strong King Gene instead of Kirby. After all, shouldn't a princess marry a king?

No one knows what became of poor Alpheus Kirby or his children. But one day the sun rose over the sawgrass and shone upon the 'Widow Kirby' and King Gene and all the little Hamiltons they had created, and the Hamilton tribe was born. If you close your eyes, you can see them there, the beautiful Indian maiden and her King, crude but deadly tomahawk tucked in his belt, on the sandy white seashell strewn shore at Lostmans River.

Another tomahawk story included in a 1944 article called "Paradise USA" tells of a young man who turns himself into the sheriff after taking care of a ruffian.

"Recently a member of the clan, a husky youth with proud, dark eyes, walked into the courthouse at Everglades City and asked to see Sheriff Roy Atkins.

"I've had a little trouble," he said, "with a smart-aleck down our way. It was about my sister. He got fresh with my sister, and now I've had a little trouble with him. You'd better go and see how he is, and then if you want me I'll be at Lostmans River."

The smart aleck, when they found him, was a sight. The brother had worked on him with the family hatchet. They took 118 stitches in his carcass and learned that the girl's brother had told the truth about the cause of the battle. It isn't only in the Everglades that wrongs to sisters are wiped out in private battle. The sheriff never sent for the brother."[3]

The Missing Schoolteacher

The day came when the supervisor at the Monroe County school board decided he needed to send a teacher out to

---

[3] Seabrook, William. Paradise U.S.A. *American Weekly*, 1944.

Lostmans River. There were an awful lot of children out there, and it was the state's duty to ensure that all of the children had a proper education. King Gene was not happy about this development. The women were doing just fine teaching the little ones how to read and write. "All's they need to know is the Lord's Prayer and Ten Commandments," he told the officials.

This, of course, did not stop the government from doing what the government does. They sent out a crew of men to build a small schoolhouse on one of the islands. They interviewed a few schoolteachers and found a young man willing to take on the challenge of schooling in the swamps. The sturdy men erected the little schoolhouse, and the schoolteacher set himself up in it. He was ready to spread some knowledge. The crew shook his hand, jumped on the next boat, and headed back to the mainland.

No one thought to check in on the schoolteacher. Sometimes when we tell this story, we call him the 'little schoolteacher,' sometimes he is not a he, he is a she. Tales change with each telling it seems. In any case, the end of the story is always pretty much the same. At the end of the school term, the superintendent decided to check on the teacher, but when he sent a boat out to check on him, he was nowhere to be found. So, he sent the Coast Guard out to see what they could find.

They found the children running around as usual, climbing trees, wading in the water, squatting in the sand shucking oysters, chasing each other up palm trees and knocking down coconuts. It was like a scene from Tahiti, but there was no schoolteacher in sight. One of the men asked a little brown boy wearing only torn at the knees blue jeans, "What happened to your school building?"

The little boy just shrugged his shoulders and ran off to find his Papa.

"Where is the schoolteacher?" they asked King Gene.

Gene, like his boy, shrugged, bored with the conversation. "Run off somewheres." He was a man of few words.

"And the schoolhouse?"

King Gene looked the man dead in the eye. "Didn't see no reason to waste good lumber, so we used it for other things."

Now, everyone knew the rumors about that tomahawk and that bone pile, so the two Coast Guard men decided it was getting late and it might be best to just move on along. King Gene and his princess watched their boat pop pop pop right on out of Lostmans.

The Seminole Influence

There are many tales in our family about Charlie Tigertail and other Seminoles who lived, worked, and played with the Ten Thousand Islands residents. Charlie Tigertail in particular is mentioned often as the Seminole Chief of that time period.

According to the Seminoles of today, however, there really were not any 'chiefs' in the tribe. The people tended to look up to one particular man at any given time as the leader. These leaders were charismatic and influential among the tribe and in dealing with the white population.

Charlie's brother, Jack, was one such influential 'chief' in the early part of the 20th century. Charlie's main claim to fame was that he was the first Seminole to open and run a trading post, a fact that put him into frequent contact (and friendship) with Ted Smallwood, owner of the main trading post in Chokoloskee.

Jack Tigertail's image was actually used by the city of Hialeah in 1921 to attract tourists. Tigertail was popular with the tribe, and his counsel was sought out often. Unfortunately, with popularity comes those who want to tear that down. Tigertail was fatally shot in the back by a white man on March

8, 1922. It is reported that his last words were, "Me going on long sleep. White man, he shot me."

Everyone agrees that the Hamilton family had a good relationship with the Seminoles in the islands. My father told me that it was common for the whole Hamilton tribe to disappear once a year into the interior islands, always about the same time that the Indians in the area quietly slipped into the wilds, whole clans, dugouts cutting through the sawgrass, men, women, and children fading into the moss for weeks at a time. For this short period, the islands were quieter than usual, just the hum of ever-present insects, bird calls, and alligators splashing into the swamp waters. Where did they all go? The annual Corn Dance perhaps?

Rubbing Down with Sausage Oil

Eugene Mervin

"I also saw several times when the Indian uprising in the Everglades….I'm going back now 1933, 32, 31..when they was in their war tribe...having a war up these rivers and things, they'd come sailing down Lostmans River in their canoes. And they'd all have the braves painted in some kind of war paint. I remember this as a young boy. And they would come to my daddy (King Gene) and they'd say to him, "What shall we do?" in the Indian language.

And my dad said, "Don't start any war 'cause I'll have to take you to Key West."

My daddy did not have no jurisdiction over these Indians at that time 'cause the government had all charge of 'em. But he was trying to explain to them that whatever they did, the law wouldn't approve of it. So, they loved my dad.

They used to go in my dad's store at that time and my dad... if you're an old person, anybody over 60 years old could remember... back those days you bought sausage in 48 lb cans, what they call 'oil sausage.' It was already cooked, prepared, but they was in oil, peanut oil or whatever, not soybean oil but peanut oil. The Indians would buy a 48 lb can of these sausages and they'd take 'em to their camp which was on our property, fires going, they was dancing, having a good time. They'd stick their hands in and dig the sausages out and take the oil and rub it all over their body.

And they said that was sacred to them. That was God's gift to them because they had a way of living 'cause they had no meat except the wildlife. But they'd say that sausage was a gift from heaven that they lived on. It's what they needed, and they wiped their bodies down in oil and whatever. And when they left my dad's place at Lostmans River, they went away happy, no war, no animosity in their hearts whatsoever. I think that's what made everything okay."

Wrestling Lucy Tiger

Eugene Mervin

"Going back to the Indian generations, my dad was only about 5 foot 10 inches tall but he always weighed over 200 lbs., not heavy, but just a strong man. This Indian buck was 6 foot, his name was Lucy Tiger, weighed about 180 lbs. He always wanted to wrastle my daddy, and my dad said no, him being a deputy sheriff, he didn't wanna do this thing. And Lucy Tiger kept insisting, and I've seen my dad pick this man up bodily, hold him up in the air, spin him around, and throw him down on the ground. But this Indian wouldn't give up, he kept coming back. I've seen it happen a dozen times.

My dad'd say, "Look Lucy, go on about your business, you're drinking."

And he come run at my daddy, and my dad'd stand flat footed on his feet and pick this man up, like a wrastler, and pick him up over his head, spin him around and throw 'em down on the ground. It'd kill me. Ya know? But this young Indian buck, ya know, they that way. They're nice guys over there."

Arresting E.J. Watson

Eugene Mervin

"I would like to say one thing going back a few years because you heard me say earlier that my daddy and Watson had a lot of encounters or whatever. When the sheriff over to Monroe County come over to arrest Watson, he didn't arrest him. He was in a field for eight days hoeing cane.

Well at that time, my grandfather (Richard Hamilton) was doing his own work and the United States Marshal's office called him and deputized him to arrest Watson. He arrested Watson. He's the only man that ever arrested Watson and took him to Key West. He put him on a sailing schooner and took him on down there.

On the night going to Key West, he told Watson, "You know, Watson, you got to have a night shift of steering this boat to Key West. When you see the lights of Key West, you call me."

And Watson said, "I'll take it."

Grandpa said, "I'll tell you something, Watson, I sleep with one eye open 'cause my dad was part Cherokee Indian."

Then Grandpa told Ed Watson, "If you make the first move, you'll never see Key West again."

So, he took him to Key West, and had the authorities to lock Watson up. About four or five days later, his henchman, Cox and several other ones, broke him out of Key West jail. They sailed back to Chatham Bend River where Watson had lived and just shortly after that was when he got mobbed and killed by Henry Shorty... on Chokoloskee Island."

Pelicans & Ghosts

<u>Junior</u>

"In the early 1930s we lived on Wood Key down in the Ten Thousand Islands. Besides us, there were several other families, all kin. Our house was in the middle of the Key and down from our house was white sandy beach. My brother, Francis, and I always liked to play and splash around in the water there. Along about this time Daddy and his cousin went hunting and disappeared, never to return.

Francis and I were playing in the water one day when more than a dozen pelicans swam right up to us within touching distance. They had never done anything like that before. Uncle Andrew[4] grabbed us out of the water and rushed us into the house and told Mama to keep us inside. He thought the pelicans were going to take us away to Daddy."

Panther Hunting

<u>Junior</u>

Sitting here in my camp in the middle of five acres of land, surrounded by live oak, green oak, pine trees, palmetto palms and gopher holes, brings back memories of my youth. We fished most every night, weather permitting. Bill Parker, my stepdad, always would take me along for company and help. I was around ten or eleven years old at that time. We left the Key and poled our skiff out into the bay east of Mormon Key, hunting and listening for mullet. When mullet jumps out of the water, then goes back in, it makes a most distinct sound by flipping its tail. You can tell by the flipping of the tail if the fish is a mullet or a catfish. We poled around and listened for about two or three hours, but we didn't hear anything.

---

[4] It is not clear how "Andrew" is related.

We were poling along the mangrove swamp and came to Henery (sic) Creek when Bill told me, "Junior, get the net anchor and throw it over into the mangroves when we start up the creek. We're going to zig-zag our net up the creek and hopefully we'll catch a few big soggies." Soggies are real big mullet that live in the swamps. When you eat them, they taste real muddy.

When we finished laying our net in the creek, we made coffee. We always carried a metal bucket half full of sand and a small amount of wood so we could build a small fire and make coffee. We called it *Gallon Can Coffee*. While the coffee was cooking, Bill whispered to me, "Don't talk or move. I see a panther."

He picked up his 22 rifle and aimed it. I looked to the right where he aimed and saw a big brown panther with his front paws up on the mangrove roots. You could see his big eyes shining, looking into the carbide light. Bill fired a shot and the panther fell and screamed. It sounded like the scream of a terrified woman.

Bill dropped his rifle, jumped in the back of the skiff and said to me, "Junior, give me a hand roping in the net." When you rope in a net, it means you pull your net aboard without clearing the fish from it.

When we were back out in the bay, I asked Bill, "Why didn't we get that panther and get its hide?"

He said, "Son, when you find one panther, he has a mate close by, and I didn't have time to find another bullet."

We went on back to Mormon Key, pulled our skiff up on the beach and went to bed. Next morning at daybreak, we cleared our net. We had caught very few fish that night. To this day I often wonder if we killed that panther, or if he licked his wound and lived on into a ripe ole age."

Fig. 12.2 William David Parker

Chapter 13

TROUBLE IN PARADISE

Tourists, entrepreneurs, and developers became even more of a regular presence in the islands. As many of the permanent residents there knew their way through the hundreds of canals, many of them served as guides to these guests. What the visitors did not see however was what was going on behind the picturesque scenery and exotic wildlife.

The Hamilton and Gomes family, along with just about everyone else in the islands, had their hands into something other than fishing, farming, and guiding. For the inhabitants of the islands, moonshining was as common as knowing the tides. Smuggling human cargo was another way of making some money, although I found no evidence of the Hamilton or Gomes families being involved in that venture. And then there was, of course, the frequent encroachment of one family by another on favored trapping and fishing grounds. The newspapers were rife with tales of stabbings, shootings, and missing persons in and around the Everglades.

Moonshine

From 1919 to 1933, the manufacture and sale of alcohol was outlawed with the passing of the Volstead Act. In 1922, Chokoloskee was home to families fishing, hunting, and farming. The Indians occasionally would stop to by sell alligator skins, and the islands' moonshiners did a steady business. Down at Lostmans River, the Hamiltons had a nice little side business making and running moonshine. The Farm provided the ingredients for several types of spirits: whisky, brandy, moonshine.

In 1961, a newspaper article shared Florida's railroad commissioner, Jerry Carter's explanation on how to make the four basic types of liquor in West Florida.

"The rum and 'shine are made in a copper still, just like you would corn-likker.

"The skeet is made in a 54-gallon oil or gasoline drum, and you can take a good stiff drink of that and you just go ske-e-e-et!

"It has a similar effect on you that this likker the Negroes make which is called 'hen-likker.' They say you take a drink of that and 'lay' right there!

"The shinny is made in an old-fashioned iron wash pot. You fill the pone one quarter full of well fermented mash or beer. Then you take a wool blanket, fold it and lay it over the top with a little iron hoop around it to keep it from sagging.

"Then you kindle a slow fire under the pot, not enough to make it boil up into the blanket, but just enough to make it simmer.

"The alcohol, being lighter than water, evaporates first, and eventually your blanket becomes thoroughly saturated and you take it off and wring it out and you'll have about a quart to a quart and a half of the best shinny you've ever drunk in your life!

"The only trouble we have in making shinny down here now is that these dang Yankees who make the blankets and ship them down here insist on putting some kind of colored border on each one of them.

"You just can't buy a good white blanket anymore."[1]

A descendent of Leon, George Hamilton   shared the Hamilton family's recipe for homemade brandy: "You need 25

---

[1] Meiklejohn, Don. "Some Moonshine Recipes" 4.

lbs of fruit with meat, like mangoes and cherries, and 25 lbs of sugar, 25 gal. of water and 2 packets of yeast. Cut the fruit up, get the water warm enough to melt the sugar and activate the yeast. Cover loosely for 27 days, strain through cheesecloth as you pour into your pot. With a fairly decent still you'll get 5 gal. of 150 proof brandy. That was the family recipe. Very, very simple."[2]

Walter's stills provided the product. A.W. and Julian Dimock describe the setup of a typical still in their 1908 book *Florida Enchantments*:

"The big iron kettle over the fire was fitted with a wooden top, deftly fashioned from a section of a cypress tree three feet in diameter, the stump of which served as a table within the glade. An iron pipe led from the cypress cover of the kettle through a wooden box of water, and from its projecting end poured a tiny stream of the potent product of the still."[3]

Leon used the *Abigail* to get the liquor to Key West for sale. In 1941, five gallons of 'white lightning' sold for $20.[4]

Mobster Al Capone reportedly produced moonshine to keep a nearby saloon jumping in the 1930s. Descendent William Leo Gomes remarks, "Al Capone was a friend and business associate of my grandfather (King Gomes). Someone has a photo of Al and my grandfather posing together at a saloon in Cuba." I wish I could find that photo!

Paul Gomes says,

> "The smuggling was rum, they all brought rum and gin and all that stuff. You got to remember; these people weren't that stupid. They knew that nobody could buy booze, so everybody in

---

[2] Hamilton, George. Personal Interview, 2019.

[3] Dimock. "Chapter 5, Makers of Moonshine," 77

[4] "'White Lightning' Hit By High Living Cost"

Europe was sending it over and they'd send it to Cuba or the Bahamas or somewhere and then the smugglers would go over and get it and bring it in. It's been the same since time began. There's a market open, fill it. When they got it here, Al Capone or somebody would have trucks load it up, take it to north, sell it in all the speakeasys. You know, a lot of smuggling came from Canada too, there's a lot of booze came in through there. It was a very hard life for all those people, including me."

King Gene kept the law in the islands during that time period, so it made making and hauling illegal liquor a bit easier for the Hamilton brothers. In the early 30s, Charles Whidden, Leon's son in law, got caught in Fort Myers with a boatload of moonshine, and that was enough for the Hamilton men. The stories passed down from the elders say that there was no more making moonshine after that. They destroyed the majority of the stills, leaving behind just the remnants of their foray into the moonshine business. Some say the remains of Walter's 100 gallon still are still out there on Lostmans River somewhere.

Development

Along with smuggling alcohol, the residents of the islands were able to add some extra income to their family coffers by acting as guides to developers, tourists, and potential homesteaders from around the world. The Hamilton and Gomes brothers are recorded in several places as working as guides to take people to view the land that they had purchased. It was quite a trek involving trains, boats, and hiking to get to their little lots of 'paradise'.

One of the largest promotions was Poinciana. Tebeau says, "Lostman's River was the scene of one of Florida's most spectacular real estate promotions in the middle twenties. The Tropical Development Company, a Miami concern, acquired three sections of land astride the mouth of Lostman's River, and laid out on paper—but did not survey—Poinciana, as a future subdivision."[5]

The primary means of getting the word out about Poinciana was through advertising in the newspapers. Several of these advertisements included the Hamilton and Gomes family as models of how successful homesteading in the Everglades could be.

Tropical Development sold thousands of lots to hopeful homesteaders. In 1925, 50 foot lots were advertised by Miami developers at $100 and corner lots for $250.[6] By 1929, agents around the country were charged with fraud. The Miami News reports, "Promises to construct a town in a remote section of the state are alleged to have been made by the men and never fulfilled."[7] Needless to say, Poinciana never materialized.

---

[5] Tebeau, Charlton W. *Man in the Everglades*, 112-113

[6] "Fishing at Poinciana." *The Miami News*, 15.

[7] "*Agents Held for Frauds.*" The Miami News. 9 Feb 1929, 2.

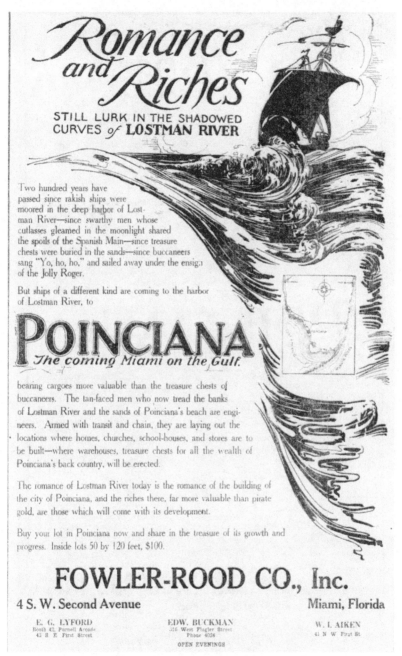

Fig. 13.1. Advertisement for Poinciana[8]

---

[8] *The Miami News.* 23 Oct 1925.

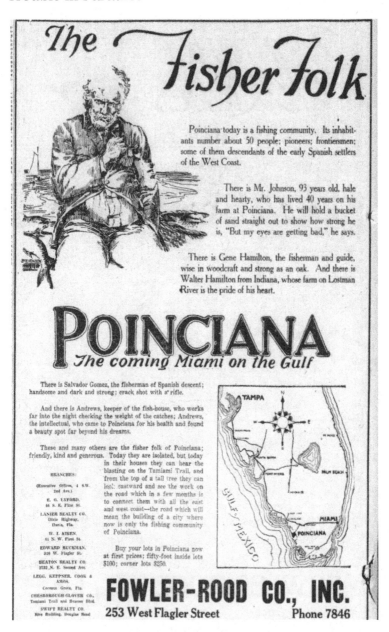

Fig. 13.2 Advertisement for Poinciana.[9]

---

[9] *The Miami News.* 3 Jan 1926.

Fig. 13.3 Advertisement for Poinciana.[10]

[10] *The Tampa Tribune.* 23 Feb 1926.

Fish Wars & Fights

The residents of Lostmans were quiet men who kept to themselves as much as possible. Making a living and feeding their families took up the majority of their time. As such, they were protective over their favored fishing, hunting, and trapping grounds. The other fights among the clan were domestic and often involved fights over women. Most disputes were handled quickly and quietly, whether that be resolutions that were deemed legal or not is not something we ruminate on. Everyone handled their business, and when that failed, the elder Hamiltons stepped in to handle it for them.

The newspapers from that era offer bits and scraps of stories that many of the descendants have never heard. From this distance, we will never know the whole story and are left to speculate. One such scrap is a small mention of a kidnapping. Salvador Gomes and William 'Buddy' Hamilton were charged with kidnapping and Rosalie Gomes was charged with "aiding and abetting" in 1926. No other details were given other than that the accused had not been apprehended and the case was set to continue.

As a researcher, you can spend weeks following up this one lead, but as of this writing, I have found no more mention of the alleged kidnapping.[11] I did spend hours scrolling through microfiche at the Monroe County Courthouse in Key West, but only found the incident mentioned on a court docket listing the three of them, the alleged crime, and their court date, January 1926. Still, this government document served to confirm for me that the three were charged and went to court. I checked with the Civil Court in Key West for arrest records or case closings, but I was told that their records only extended

---

[11] "Cases Continued," 3

back to 1948. Once again, we are left to speculate who was kidnapped and why. This particular 'family secret' has not joined the oral memory banks of those I have spoken with about the family. Again, some secrets are best left secret.

The families had occasional run-ins with the bad boys of the islands. William Rewis and his cohorts were well known in the region for their criminal activities and violent tendencies. In 1929, Sheriff Cleveland Niles from Key West and his guide, Salvador Gomez[12], were lost for a few days in the islands after searching for the Rewis gang. Rewis was accused of stabbing Gene Hamilton in several places and slashing the throat of Gene's son, Josie, the deaf-mute, while they were all at a dance on Lostmans River. Rewis also allegedly hit Rebecca Hamilton over the head with a boat hook and bit "a piece of her nose off" and assaulted her daughter, Irene.

The Hamilton family claimed that William Rewis and his gang were poaching on Hamilton property, and that is what started the affair. Rewis had been captured and taken to Key West, but Sheriff Niles and Gomes continued to search for the

rest of the gang along Shark River. A search party was called to look them for them. They needn't have worried. Gomes was often mistaken for a 'Seminole guide' as he knew his way around those islands as well as the Seminoles did. The two turned up four days later, totally unaware that they had been 'lost.'

Fig. 13.4 Joaquin 'King' Gomes

---

[12] Gomes (the correct spelling) is most often spelled 'Gomez' in older documents.

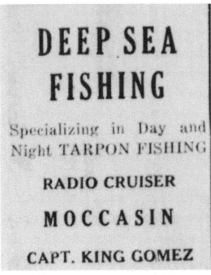

DEEP SEA FISHING

Specializing in Day and Night TARPON FISHING

RADIO CRUISER

MOCCASIN

CAPT. KING GOMEZ

Fig. 13.5 Advertisement King used for his charter business

The family made frequent runs in the Gulf with produce and, most likely, moonshine. King Gomes and Robert Hamilton, Leon's son, went missing in April 1930 while out on a run. After they were found, Gomes said they had run out of fuel. The tanker *Pioneer* had spotted them in the Gulf on Friday and offered to tow them to Cuba. Officers on that tanker reported that Gomes offered them "a couple of quarts" in exchange for fuel, but Gomes later denied that. At any rate, officers of the *Pioneer* stated that the pair declined their offer of a tow, another story that Gomes denies. Shortly after the *Pioneer* left the two, the tanker *Portreath* came across the small boat which was by then floundering in the increasingly rough sea. That time the two accepted rescue and boarded the tanker for a lift to Cuba. Their boat was left where it was, and the *Portreath* reported to the Naval Station that the boat had been abandoned and was "a menace to navigation."[13]

On Turkey Key one night in August 1931, Josie Hamilton stopped by John Bodiford's houseboat to ask if he had any gas. Now, Bodiford supposedly was sweet on Josie's girl and had made some improper advances towards her. So, when Josie and his people showed up at his home, he figured Josie's girl had told on him. He ordered Josie and the others off his boat.

---

[13] "King Gomez and Companion Back." and "Two Key Westers Picked up Drifting in Gulf Stream are Taken into Cuba."

Then he went to get his knife. His nephew, Charles, fearing trouble, jumped Josie and the fight was on. John Bodiford appeared with a gun and fired a shot that struck Josie's sister,

Helen (Ellen), in the hand. The bullet tore straight through her hand and buried itself in Josie's belly. The trial, with John Bodiford charged with attempt to murder and Charles Bodiford charged as an accessory, went on throughout the fall.

Fig. 13.6 Joseph 'Josie' Hamilton

The Key West Citizen reported that "Young Hamilton (Josie) is well known to a number of Key West people having lived here for several months with his parents, who came here to attend a trial, following several attempts on the life of the father (King Gene). They stayed here until conditions became more settled in that section (Lostman River)."[14] We know that King Gene was feared and respected in the islands, but this is another instance where we may never know the whole story.

Considering the troubled times, a population of people who lived outside of mainstream society, and the fact that Gene was a deputy, it is not surprising that attempts had been

---

[14] "Deaf Mute Shot, Seriously Hurt in This County," 1.

made to get rid of him. Deputy Gene Hamilton didn't exactly turn a blind eye to fish and game violations. But he was known for casually mentioning where he would be on a given day. Men in the area knew to avoid that area then. Gene took his job seriously. He had a job to do, and if you didn't heed him, he had no problems with doing that job. It is a testament to how highly Gene was thought of that the manager of the Mercedes Hospital offered him and his family a place to sleep and food during the Bodiford trial.

These fights and feuds amongst the residents of the islands intensified as commercial fishermen from around the country moved into the region. The term 'fish wars' was a journalistic term used to describe the feuds taking place amongst commercial and local fishermen in regions such as Alaska and Florida. In the Everglades and the Florida Keys, the term was used by local authorities and the U.S. Coast Guard. The Coast Guard's jurisdiction began 12 miles out from land, while local authorities were responsible for what took place inside that range and inland.

By January 1932, the fish wars in Monroe and Collier counties were nearing a climax. The fishermen in Monroe County complained frequently to the local authorities that outsiders were poaching on their fishing grounds. The unwritten law in the islands was that everyone claimed their 'spot' and others left them to it. The local authorities could do nothing. No one actually owned any particular fishing ground. Still, the threats of violence between the locals and the outsiders got worse and everyone knew trouble was coming soon.

The climax arrived when, early in January, in Key West, someone stole and set fire to the *Eulalia*, a 65-foot fishing boat owned by Commander Leroy Reinburg from the Miami Fish company. With local authorities claiming there was 'no violence' taking place in Monroe County, the frustrated

Reinburg called for help from the Coast Guard, stating that "nothing short of government aid can cope with the present situation." The commander ordered his men to patrol the waters around Key West and protect the local fishermen from harm.

Deputy Sheriff Gene Hamilton spent his time fishing, working at 'the farm,' negotiating with the Seminoles, keeping the peace among the residents, and occasionally turning a blind eye to the moonshiners and smugglers. As the feuds and fights intensified, Gene found himself facing a very personal tragedy, a loss so great that it threatened to finally break him.

The Racial Issue

By the 1930 census, the census takers were listing the Hamilton clan as 'Neg' (Negro).

In April 23, 1930, Gene and Rebecca were living on Pearl Street in Key West and listed on the census as White. Their children, Ellen, Ethel, Irene, Roy, Eugene, Jr. were also listed as White. Gene's nephew, Robert (White) lived with them.

Two months later, on June 26, they were listed on the census as living at Poundiana Point (sic)[15], near Lostmans River. Gene owned the property, valued at $500. On this census, they and their children were listed as Negro. The rest of the Hamilton clan were scattered around them on the nearby islands: Richard, Walter, Leon, Buddy and Florinda, Salvador Gomes. All with the exception of Salvador, who was listed as White even though he was Portuguese, were listed as Negro. Salvador was married to Rosalie Hamilton, and she and Salvador's children were all listed as Negro. All owned the properties they lived on at Lostmans River and Mormon Key.

---

[15] Most likely a misspelling of *Poinciana,* which is mentioned earlier in this chapter.

Race chosen by association? Why would Rebecca Johnson and Florinda Gomes be listed as Negro? Neither had any ties to slavery or African heritage. Florinda was part Portuguese.

On the June 1930 census, I found Eva Hamilton, daughter of Leon, listed with her husband, Charles Whidden, and she was listed as white. So, this is just another example of how the whole race question lay in the eyes of the perceiver. If everyone listed in Leon's household was Negro then it stands to reason that Eva would be as well. But she is living nearby with her 'white' husband, so the census taker lists as her 'white.'

Again, the question of race was often problematic, this distinction that was ever present and dictated how the family was treated by the other islanders.

Chapter 14

THE MISSING BOYS

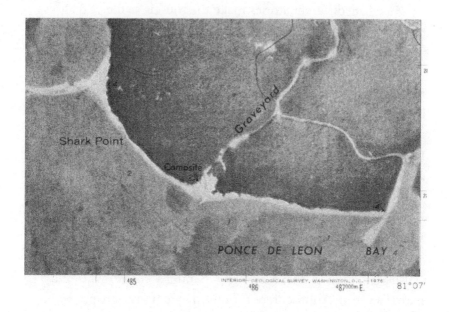

Map 14.1 Shark Point and Graveyard Creek, 2019

"Graveyard Creek was so named because of a double murder rumored to have been committed there. Both of the families involved lived in the Everglades City and Lostman's area at the time, and relatives of these families still live near Everglades City."[1]

---

[1] Truesdell, William G. *A Guide to the Wilderness Waterway - Everglades, Florida*, 50.

In the Glades, tempers were flaring and reaching the
boiling point by the summer of 1931. Disputes over
fishing rights and trapping violations had created mini-
feuds amongst the residents of the islands.

Leon Hamilton was attacked by an unknown person
wielding a hatchet. The official count of his wounds was 18
and he remained in serious condition for some time. Leon bore
the scars of the attack, which left the right side of his face
disfigured, for the rest of his life.

As usual, different stories make the rounds as the years go
by. I heard one story that claims King Gomes was the one
wielding the hatchet. Most of the Hamiltons were positive it
was a Santini, but this was never proven. Why the Hamilton's
feel it was one of the Santini family can only be attributed to
the hostilities circulating throughout the region at that time.

Most accounts say that Adolphus Santini was a Corsican
from Charleston, South Carolina. He came to the region
around 1870 with his family and took over the Chokoloskee
area when John Weeks, who settled there, moved on.
Adolphus Santini became legendary as one in the long list of
Edgar J. Watson's victims. Apparently, E. J. Watson marched
across the street from the barbershop where he had just
finished getting a shave and cut Santini's throat with the
barber's razor. (Another report of the incident says it happened
at an auction house.) Santini survived and declined to
prosecute Watson saying that he and Watson were friends.

According to one news report, "...having missed the jugular
vein, Santini recovered and refused to prosecute, saying they
were 'friends.' But Sheriff Frank Knight went after him
(Watson) anyway, pretending he had a warrant. He was met as
usual by Watson, rifle in hand, and ordered to stand off. When
Knight called that he had a warrant, Watson called back that
he would report at Key West when he had his crops in, and so

he did. Nothing came of it, for lack of a complainant."[2] Knowing Watson's reputation by this time, it is no wonder that Santini chose to turn the other cheek.

William 'Buddy' Hamilton, my grandfather and eldest child of Gene Hamilton disappeared in February 1932. Buddy was the first to join the Gomes and Hamilton clans together with his marriage to Florinda Gomes. They had two sons and another on the way when he disappeared one day with his cousin, Robert Joseph, on a hunting trip. Buddy was barely 28 years old.

Fig. 14.1 William 'Buddy' Hamilton

---

[2] Stout, Wesley. *Barber's Razor Used on Throat In Florida Keys, 11*

Robert, the son of Leon Hamilton and Sarah Elizabeth Johnson was only 21. Robert was married to Lola Lee Callaway and they had one daughter, Lula May.

Fig. 14.2 Robert Hamilton

There has some debate from family members as to whether the photo of Robert shown here is indeed Robert Hamilton or his brother, Henry.

Fig. 14.3 Paul Gomes says, "Authorities brought a teacher down to Lostmans but Buddy knew more than the teacher, so they fired the teacher and Buddy taught the class." Buddy is on the far left of this photo.

Ernie

"The story has it that William had a brilliant mind. Of course, everything is relative. He may very well have been smarter than the average trooper in that area. The settlers brought in a teacher from the mainland when William was a teenager. He learned everything the teacher had to teach in a short time and the teacher told him, "I can't teach you anymore, you've got all that I have.""

William played, very well, by ear, the guitar, banjo, mandolin, and the fiddle. He built an animal trap from which an animal could not escape. He patented it and was offered $1,700 for it, which he did not take. He built a carburetor out of spare parts while fishing. In those days a car backfired considerably and continuously because the charge and the gas to the spark plugs were improperly timed. William designed a distributor that would prevent misfiring. I still have those drawings. There is some evidence that he hired lawyers in Fort Myers to represent him, but someone beat him to the patent office with the same solution to the problem. That the lawyers used his ideas could not be proven.

Piecing together the few newspaper accounts of Buddy and Robert's disappearance yields the date of disappearance as January 15, 1932. The story in the newspapers say that King Gene told them that he was with Buddy and Robert at the mouth of Little Shark River when a mob came after them.

It is not clear how they all got separated, but King Gene was able to escape. King Gene told authorities that "he left the two boys ... at the mouth of Little Shark River" and that "when he left the boys a 'mob' was after him and he feared that they had killed the boys."[3] Fearing for the boy's lives, King Gene asked the local authorities to help with the search, but no help was forthcoming.

---

[3] "Father Fears Mob Murdered Missing Boys," 14

After searching for nearly three weeks, King Gene appealed to the Coast Guard for help in finding the missing boys. Reports from others looking say that the men's skiff was in the water, but there was no sign of Buddy or Robert. Commander LeRoy Reinburg of the Coast Guard sent a boat piloted by Boatswain Leo P. Toolin to Little Shark River to look for the pair. It would take him roughly 12 hours to reach the river from Sanibel Island. Reinburg didn't think the men's disappearance had anything to do with the fish wars that were an ongoing trial to him, but the mention of a 'mob' bothered him. As Toolin was very familiar with the islands because of the fishing conflicts, Reinburg was confident that if anyone could discover what had happened, Toolin could.[4]

On the way to Shark River, Toolin was sidetracked by a Cuban fishing schooner that he suspected was smuggling rum into the islands. Because the schooner was within the 12-mile limit, Toolin was responsible for stopping to search it. He found nothing illegal, just a boat full of grouper. This search cost precious hours, but he finally resumed his trek to Shark River. Toolin had no luck finding any evidence of foul play on Shark River or Lostmans River, however. He planned to return another time to check out other creeks near the area.

The search continued for several agonizing weeks for the missing men, but all that was ever found was the skiff they were using that day. By February 13, the Coast Guard reported that the fish wars in Monroe County were over and the search for William 'Buddy' and Robert was discontinued.

FISH WAR CONCLUDED AS BOATS MOVE AWAY

"Indication that the 'fish war' in Monroe county has ended was seen Friday in radio

---

[4] Ibid.

reports received by Commander LeRoy Reinburg, commanding Base 21, U. S. Coast Guard. These reports from the patrol boats operating near Key West said that all fishing boats had left Monroe county waters for Tavernier Key in Dade county along Barnes Sound. The Coast Guard patrol boat 181 has been dispatched to Shark River to relieve the 295 which has been there for about two weeks searching for two boys supposed to have been lost. No trace of the boys was ever found.[5]"

On February 21st, the Key West Citizen reported that, "Robert and William Hamilton, the young men reported lost in the Shark River Section have been seen. They were said to be in a sailboat going to Tampa." This small paragraph reverberated through my family almost a century later. It is the first that we had heard of the possibility that the two might still be alive. After speaking with family, reading King Gene's testimony, and considering a deathbed confession that would come many years later, we mostly discount this theory that the two boys ran off.

Great-grandson of King Gene, Paul Gomes tells this story, "When I was in grade school in Everglades, I was in school with Floyd Brown and believed the Brown brothers killed Uncle Buddy and Robert Hamilton. Floyd and I used to fight every day after school about this. When Floyd's father finally died, he came to me and told me his father on his deathbed admitted killing them!" Another story says that Buddy and Robert were stealing from someone's traps and got caught. Still others believed the theory that the boys had just run off. And then there is the story my own father grew up with, that the

---

[5] "Fish War Concluded as Boats Move Away," 24.

killer confessed to the murders while getting drunk in a bar one day.

Fig. 14.4 Salvador Gomes on the left, William Joseph 'Buddy' Hamilton on the right, seated is Eugene Joseph 'King Gene' Hamilton. King Gene was a lawman for a while in the islands.

Gomes says, "Papa never stopped looking for Buddy. He died a broken-hearted man." Buddy's wife, Florinda Gomes, gave birth to a son on September 24, 1932, Ernest Eugene Hamilton, my father. A year later, Florinda married Bill Parker in Charlotte county. My father, Ernest, and his brothers, Bill and Francis were raised for a while by Parker. They lived on

Wood Key and the nearby islands. Parker and Florinda divorced in 1942, and Florinda and the boys moved to Key West.

These are the tales that circulate 86 years later. Old wounds still fester among some of the families. People can speculate, but when it comes down to truth there are only the people who were there who can tell it – and voices buried in the Florida Everglades keep their secrets.

Fig. 14.5 William 'Buddy' Hamilton on Lostmans River, circa 1927

Fig. 14.6 Ellen and William 'Buddy' Hamilton

Fig. 14.7 William 'Buddy' Hamilton

Fig. 14.8 Florinda Gomes Hamilton and William 'Bill' Parker

Fig. 14.9 Florinda Gomes Hamilton Parker with her and Buddy's sons. Top: Francis Salvador Theodore, Ernest Eugene. Bottom: Flo and William Joseph, Jr. (Junior).

Chapter 15

NO PLACE TO GO

Richard Hamilton was confirmed in the Catholic Church in February of 1933. He was the oldest candidate in the class, his age listed as "100 years and six months." In 1933, the Key West Citizen ran a short article about Richard. He was approximately 85 years then, but true to character, he lied as the situation suited him.

Fig. 15.1 Richard Hamilton 101 years old

Robert E. Hamilton 101 years old seeks work on Relief Roll.

"Regarded as too old to be a registrant on the relief rolls of the C.W.A. or F.E.R.A., Robert E. Hamilton feels that he could do the work required, even though he is 101 years old.

Asked if he felt equal to the tasks that might be imposed should he be called for work, Mr. Hamilton replied that he has been going strong for the past three score years and ten and then some and believes he could hold his own.

To show that he is still active and supple, this young-old centenarian danced a few steps of a jig for the benefit of *The Citizen*.[1]

Richard retreated to Key West, an old man past the centenarian mark. In 1944, coinciding with the beginning of the end of the pioneers in the Everglades, Richard passed away sitting on the dock watching his beloved river. He was buried beneath the Poinciana tree on Lostmans River.

The Key West Citizen says in his obituary, "He was sprightly long after he had passed the century mark. He walked rapidly and could be seen frequently along the shore of the Garrison Bight attending to his boat."

During this time, plans were well in motion to create Everglades National Park. Residents still living on the various keys in the area were told that they could remain in their homes as long as their homes were still standing. They were not, however, allowed to fix or repair those structures in any way. As this was impossible, many of the residents moved on. Many,

---

[1] "Robert E. Hamilton 101 years old seeks work on Relief Roll." Key West Citizen. December 15, 1933, 1.

including the Hamilton brothers, moved to Flamingo. By 1920, census records indicate that Walter, Leon, and Gene were all living in Flamingo.

By 1948, the remaining structures on the islands had been burned down by the National Park Service (NPS). Only one structure remained, as it was built from block rather than wood. Some in the family say the NPS did it on purpose to drive them out. The NPS accused the remaining residents of burning down their own houses and starting fires. However, the burnings happened, and with desperation comes flared tempers, on both sides. An NPS official wrote years before the park opened, "We believe that there will be no real conservation program until certain undesirables living in the village of Flamingo and at fishing camps along the west coast are removed. People in these "pest holes" are living off the country, taking alligators, crocodiles, waterfowl, wading birds, and fur-bearing animals...Local people at times deliberately set fire to the glades causing considerable damage."[2]

In 1950, the NPS listed the people still living at Lostmans River and called them "squatters." NPS officials stated that, "None of the fishermen who lived in houses or houseboats near the mouth of Lostmans River owned any property there." Perhaps because by that time, the government had already bought them out and run them off by hiring lawyers to find every loophole imaginable to evict the 'squatters.'

> Eugene Hamilton Sr., age 60; Eugene Hamilton, Jr., age 25; F. E. Williams, age about 60; Roy Priest, age 25; Henry Hamilton, age 42; Louis McBean, age unknown; James Addison, age unknown; Leon Hamilton, age about 60;

---

[2] Blythe, Robert W. *Wilderness on the Edge: A History of Everglades National Park*

Walter Hamilton, age 71 (possibly no longer a resident).[3]

On December 2, 1950, Leon Hamilton, "% Riggs Fish Company in Everglades" was listed among hundreds of others on the Legal Notices page of the Key West Citizen calling for the condemnation of their homes.

> "You are hereby notified that a Petition for Condemnation...has been heretofore filed in the United States District Court for the Southern District of Florida, Miami Division, whereby the United States of America seeks to acquire by condemnation under judicial process....the fee simple title to the following described lands situate, lying and being in the counties of Monroe and Dade, State of Florida, to-wit: Lands in Dade and Monroe Counties, Florida, to be acquired for the Everglades National Park..."[4]

As the deadline for final eviction loomed, the residents of Flamingo sent a letter to Superintendent Beard of the NPS asking for help.

> Everglades National Park Service -
>
> We the fishermen of Flamingo have no place to go or any place to stay. Our fish haulers have refused to bring us any groceries - gas or any other supplies. We have no other way of making a living.

---

[3] Walter Hamilton died in 1947, so this is not correct.
[4] "Notice of Condemnation," 7.

We the fishermen of Flamingo will be up with our families at the office of the Everglades National Park office [sic] at 10-o'clock Saturday - June 2, 1951 for information as to where we are to go and what to do and how to take care of our families.

We feel that if the Park Service is taking our homes and our way of making a living, we think they should give us our places here to stay as this is the only place we know how to make a living.[5]

Paul Gomes recalls the leaving of his home. I sit on Paul's back porch overlooking the water in Punta Gorda. It is early morning, the sun just rising, and the coffee brewing. The water gently bumps into the dock pilings, the occasional dragonfly darts across the water and hides in the reeds. The silent sounds of nature seem appropriate for the topic at hand. We have before us on the table photographs of our ancestors, and Paul's finger rests on the photo of his Papa, that larger than life man who dominates so much of our family story, King Gene Hamilton.

Paul speaks quietly and tells me what happened after the pioneers of the Everglades lost their home.

"In 1947 we moved from Everglades City to Naples. Daddy sold the houseboat and he bought a brand-new house in Naples on a multi-family lot for $4800. We moved up there, but we were still in Lostmans River. See, you had to get out because they made it Everglades National Park. So, you had to go out. You could still fish around some places, so we'd go

---

[5] Blythe, Robert W. *Wilderness on the Edge: A History of Everglades National Park*

down there and fish, but we didn't live there. Well, we did live there; you could tie up a boat for a month or two at a time."

Some of the family moved on to other places and found their way. Others, like King Gene, moved in with family and were never the same. Gene ended up living in a small motor home, 'a chicken coop' Paul calls it, in the back of grandson, Butterball (James William) Knowles house. He continues,

"The other families, like Papa and them, the reason he got out was the park bought him out. Because he did have a deed to his property, north Lostmans. So, they bought him out. Then he moved up to Bonita Springs, him and Gladys and whatever brood was still around. He stayed in Bonita Springs. After Gladys left him, he was a lonely old man. So, he came down and lived with us. We lived in Naples. Daddy had bought Mama that new house. And so, he come down to Naples and stayed with us for a while. The reason I remember it so well is because we was only a two bedroom house, and when he came, I had to sleep on a pallet on the floor, 'cause Papa got the bedroom. And after that, he left us and went up to live with Butterball Knowles, who lived in Iona at the time."

Paul quietly finishes, "People wanted to know what they're supposed to do. In 1948, the government came in and confiscated all their land and stopped them from making a living. The government told them to go find something else to do. They went and found something to do."

For some of the descendants of the pioneers, that something was carrying on the family tradition of smuggling, this time marijuana.

But that is another story.

Final Note: Walter Hamilton died on April 14, 1947, before the final eviction from the islands. Leon passed away on January 24, 1964. On December 27, 1966, King Gene, passed away at the age of 83 in Iona, Florida.

Index

Locations are in *italics*. Unless otherwise stated, all towns and cities listed are in Florida.

Images are in **bold**.

Bibliography

Arnold, William E. *Summer In the Winter Time*. Philadelphia: Allen, Lane & Scott printers, 1891-92. Previously issued under title: Florida; or, Summer in the winter time. Issued by Passenger department of the Ocean steamship company, "The Savannah line."

Ash, Clarke. "U-M Prof Traces White Settlers In Remote Corners of Everglades." *The Miami News*. Miami, Florida. 26 Apr 1959, Sun, Page 10. Newspapers.com.

Bachmann, J. *Birds eye view of Florida and part of Georgia and Alabama* [Map]. 1861. Digital Collection. Retrieved from https://ark.digitalcommonwealth.org/ark:/50959/1257b8532

Baptismal Certificate. Richard Hamilton. Key West Courthouse, Key West Florida.Compiled by: Mona Hamilton McMahon June 25, 1994

Barbour, G. M. *Florida for tourists, invalids, and settlers: containing practical information regarding climate, soil, and productions...routes of travel,etc., etc.,ea.* Rev. ed. New York: D. Appleton and company. 1884.

Blythe, Robert W. *Wilderness on the Edge: A History of Everglades National Park*. National Park Service/Organization of American Historians, 2017. Digital copy.

"Boat Goes After Many Witnessess. Deputies to Get Those Who Will Testify in Badiford Case. *Key West Citizen*. Sept 9, 1931.

"Bodifords' Case Went to Jury at 3 This Afternoon." *Key West Citizen*. Sept 17, 1931

"Bodiford Shooting Case: Witnesses in Badiford Case Will Be Housed In Mercedes Hospital." *Key WestCitizen*. Sept 1, 1931.

Bootlegging, Low-Bush Lightning and the Murder of Deputy Sheriff J. H. Cox & Family. https://www.coastalbreezenews.com/articles/bootlegging-low-bush-lightning-and-the-murder-of-deputy-sheriff-j-h-cox-family/

Brown, Canter, and Barbara Gray Brown. *Family Records of the African American Pioneers of Tampa and Hillsborough County*. Tampa, FL: University of Tampa Press, 2003, 103-105.

Brown, Canter. *Florida's Peace River Frontier*. Orlando: University of Central Florida Press, 1991.

Brown, Faye. *Weeks Family Connection*. Straub Publishing, Blairsville, GA, 2011.

Burr, H. A. & Disturnell, J. Disturnell's new map of the United and Canada showing all the canals, railroads, telegraph lines and principal stage routes, 1851.

Cars parked near the Collier Corporation Administration Building in Everglades City. 193-?. Black & white photoprint, 3 x 6 in. State Archives of Florida, Florida Memory. <https://www.floridamemory.com/items/show/255409>, accessed 22 October 2019.

"Cases Continued." *Key West Citizen*, June 26, 1926, p. 3

Census. Online publication - Provo, UT, USA: Ancestry.com Operations Inc, 2008.Original data - Schedules of the Florida State Census of 1885; (National Archives Microfilm Publication M845, 13 Rolls); Records of the Bureau of the Census, Record Group 29; National A

Church, A., *A Dash Through the Everglades*

Clarke, J. O. D. *Ocala, Fla.: a sketch of its history, residences, business interests, etc.*, with illustrations of picturesque scenery and portraits of leading citizens. Republic Press 1891

Copeland Papers: "History of the 10,000 Islands etc." 1927, p. 1085
http://www.naplesnative.com/CopelandPapers.htm

Covington, James W. "Exploring the Ten Thousand Islands: 1838." p. 7-14.
http://digitalcollections.fiu.edu/tequesta/files/1958/58_1_02.pdf

"Judge N. H. Decoster of Harbor View is Dead." *The Tampa Times.* 31 Oct 1912, page 3.

"Deaf Mute Shot, Seriously Hurt in This County" *Key West Citizen.* August 20, 1931, p. 1.

Deposition *N. H. DeCoster.* 22 October 1902. Case of Stephen Barrett, No. 996.404. Washington, D.C.: National Archives and Records Administration, n.d.

Deposition B. *Isom Anthony.* 18 February 1895. Case of Sarah Barrett, No. 531374. Washington, D.C.: National Archives and Records Administration, n.d.

Deposition. *J. A. Davis, chief pension examiner.* Washington, D.C.: National Archives and Records Administration, n.d.

Deposition. *N. H. DeCoster.* 22 October 1902. Case of Stephen Barrett, No. 996.404. Washington, D.C.: National Archives and Records Administration, n.d.

Deposition. *J. M. Phipps, Attorney at Law, Key West. Letter to Hon. H. Clay Evins, Commissioner of Pensions,* Washington, D. C. Dec. 11th, 1901. Washington, D.C.: National Archives and Records Administration, n.d.

Deposition. *Joseph Pinckney.* Deposition (find)

Deposition. *G. H. Watson, Letter to J.A. Davis, chief pension examiner.* October 7, 1902. Washington, D.C.: National Archives and Records Administration, n.d.

Deposition A. *James Dean.* 18 February 1896. Case of Stephen Barrett, No. 996.404. Washington, D.C.: National Archives and Records Administration, n.d.

Deposition A. *Nelson English.* 7 October 1896. Case of Stephen Barrett alias Richard Hamilton, No. 996.404. Washington, D.C.: National Archives and Records Administration, n.d.

Deposition D. *Richard Hamilton.* 18 October 1902. Case of Stephen Barrett, No. 996.404. Washington, D.C.: National Archives and Records Administration, n.d.

Deposition G. *Judson Edwards.* 12 November 1902. Case of Stephen Barrett, No. 996.404. Washington, D.C.: National Archives and Records Administration, n.d.

Deposition I. *Joseph Edwards.* 21 November 1902. Case of Stephen Barrett, No. 996.404. Washington, D.C.: National Archives and Records Administration, n.d.

Deposition K. *Henrietta Edwards Jones.* 21 November 1902. Case of Stephen Barrett, No. 996.404. Washington, D.C.: National Archives and Records Administration, n.d.

Deposition O. *F. W. Johnson.* 18 November 1902. Case of Stephen Barrett, No. 996.404. Washington, D.C.: National Archives and Records Administration, n.d.

Digital Collection. Nash, Roy. Survey of the Seminole Indians of Florida. United States Department of Interior, Indian Affairs Washington, DC, 1932.
URL: http://ufdc.ufl.edu//FS00000029/00001 Site: University of Florida

Digital Collections. Dillon, Jr., Rodney E. South Florida in 1860. *The Florida Historical Quarterly,* Vol. 60. No. 4 (Apr. 1982), pp. 440-454. Florida Historical Society.
http://www.jstor.org/stable/30149852

Dimock, A. W. & Julian A. Dimock. *Florida Enchantments*. "Chapter 5, Makers of Moonshine." Outing Publishing Company. 1908. FI07100907.
http://everglades.fiu.edu/reclaim/monographs/FI07100907.htm

Dollarhide, William, *The Census Book: A Genealogist's Guide to Federal Census Facts, Schedules and Indexes,* Heritage Quest: Bountiful, Utah, 2000.

Dovell, Junius E. The Everglades, a Florida Frontier. *Agricultural History*, Vol. 22, No. 3 (Jul., 1948), pp. 187-197. Agricultural History Society. Stable URL: http://www.jstor.org/stable/3739279

Dunbar, Seymour. *History of Travel in America*. New York: Tudor Publishing Company, 1915. p. 1105

Eckert, Edward K. "Contract Labor in Florida during Reconstruction." *The Florida Historical Quarterly*, Vol. 47, No. 1 (Jul 1968), pp. 34-50 www.jstor.org/stable/30147406

Effingham Living History Museum, Springfield Georgia. Photo credit: Karen Yvonne Hamilton, 2018.

Excursion routes for the season of 1874-5. Florida. Digital Collection. https://merrick.library.miami.edu/cdm/ref/collection/pamphlets/id/4453

"Father Fears Mob Murdered Missing Boys." *Tampa Bay Times*. 1 Feb 1932 page 14.

"Fish War Concluded as Boats Move Away." *Tampa Bay Times*. 13 Feb 1932 page 24.

"Fishing at Poinciana." *The Miami News*, 15. Newspapers.com.

Florida State Archive, Tallahassee and clerk of courts, various counties; Tallahassee, Florida; *Florida, County Marriages, 1823-1982*

Florida. Clay County. 1880 U. S. Census. Roll: 126; Family History Film: 1254126; Page: 317C; Enumeration District: 017; Image: 0224

Florida. Manatee County. 1870 U. S. Census. Township 38, Roll: M593_132; Page: 166B; Image: 338; Family History Library Film: 545631

Florida. Monroe County. Key West. 1880 U. S. Census.; Roll: 131; Page: 286D; Enumeration District: 118

Florida. Monroe County. Key West. 1880 U. S. Census. Roll: T9_131; Family History Film: 1254131; Page: 286.3000; Enumeration District: 118; Image: 0212.

Florida. Monroe County. Chokoloskee. 1900 U. S. Census. Roll: T623 174; Page: 1A; Enumeration District: 108.

Florida. Monroe County. Key Mataenabe. 1910 U. S. Census. Roll: T624_165; Page: 2A; Enumeration District: 130; Image: 1124.

Florida. Monroe County. Flamingo. 1920 U. S. Census. Roll: T625_225; Page: 1B; Enumeration District: 108; Image: 1106.

Florida. Monroe County. Flamingo. 1920 U. S. Census. Roll: T625_225; Page: 1B; Enumeration District: 108; Image: 1111

Florida. Manatee County. Manatee Town. 1920 U. S. Census. Roll: T625_226; Page: 2A; Enumeration District: 118 (Hannah Hamilton)

Florida. Monroe County. Spring Hill. 1930 U. S. Census. Roll: 325; Page: 1A; Enumeration District: 0029; Image: 1094.0; FHL microfilm: 2340060

Florida. Monroe County. Key West. 1930 U. S. Census. Roll: 325; Page: 21A; Enumeration District: 0018; Image: 986.0; FHL microfilm: 2340060

Florida. Monroe County. 1940 U. S. Census. Roll: T627_601; Page: 1A; Enumeration District: 44-36

"Florida Sheriff and Indian Guide Lost After Hunting Convict in Swamp Morass." *Tampa Bay Times.* Dec 1 1929.

Futch, Jana. Historical Archaeology of the Pine Level Site (8DE14), DeSoto County, Florida, University of South Florida, 2011. https://scholarcommons.usf.edu/cgi/viewcontent.cgi?referer=http s://www.google.com/&httpsredir=1&article=4940&context=etd

"The Future of South Florida." *The Florida Peninsula,* 14 Jul 1866.

Georgia. Effingham County. 1830 U. S. Census. Series: M19; Roll: 17; Page: 106; Family History Library Film: 0007037

Georgia. Effingham County. 1840 U. S. Census. Page: 143

Ghost Towns. http://www.ghosttowns.com/states/fl/pinelevel.html Accessed Dec 31 2018.

Gomes, PaulPersonal Interview, 2018.

Gorton, Gary. *Ante Bellum Transportation Indices.* The Wharton School, University of Pennsylvania. Philadelphia, PA., August 1989. p. 26 http://faculty.som.yale.edu/garygorton/documents/AnteBellumTr ansportationIndices.pdf

Gray, Richard. Miami Weather Bureau Record, page 412.

Hamilton, George. Personal Interview, 2019.

Hamilton, Richard. Interview by JA Davis, Special Examiner, 18 October 1902. Case of Stephen Barrett, No. 996.404. Washington, D.C.: National Archives and Records Administration, n.d.

Hamilton, Ernest E. *Momma, I Tried.* Self-published.

Hamilton, Eugene M. Audio recording, 1994.

Hamilton, George. Local History: Richard/Robert Edward (R.E.) Hamilton. The Mullet Rapper Volume IX Issue #236, May 8-21, 2015, Snook Publications, Everglades City, FL. p. 9.

Hamilton, William J. Letters to Karen Y. Hamilton, 1990.

Hawkins, Betty. "Santinis Plotted at Corse." *News-Press,* Fort MyersFlorida. 28 Mar 1970, p. 10.

Historical Insights. Dawes Commission. Ancestry.com. https://www.ancestry.com/contextux/historicalinsights/dawes-commission/persons/1766881516:1030:3370971

Homan, Lynn M. and Thomas Reilly. *Key West.* Arcadia Publishing, Nov 9, 2000

Image Archives of the Historical Map & Chart Collection. Office of Coast Survey/National Ocean Service/NOAA. Sept 9 1861.

Ingraham, J.E., Diary

"The Islands Off the Southern Coast of Florida." *The Pensacolian.* 17 Jan 1885, pg 2

Johnson, C. (1918). The Everglades. *From Highways and Byways of Florida.* New York, NY: The Macmillan Company. http://etc.usf.edu/lit2go/70/florida-essays-and-poems/4358/the-everglades/

Kaye, Ken. "Solving mystery of 'Lost City' in Everglades." *Sun Sentinel,* May 18, 2014. http://www.sun-sentinel.com/local/broward/fl-lost-city-20140517-story.html

"Key West in Days Gone By." *Key West Citizen.* February 21, 1942, Page 2.

"Key West in Days Gone By." *Key West Citizen.* February 21, 1942, p. 2

Key West Courthouse, Key West Florida. Compiled by Mona Hamilton McMahon June 25, 1994.

Key West Directory 1923. Ancestry.com. *U.S. City Directories, 1822-1995* [database on-line]. Provo, UT, USA: Ancestry.com Operations, Inc., 2011.

"King Gomez and Companion Back." *Key West*

Land Warrant. Land Records of Obadiah Edwards' property in Springfield, GA. 23 Mar 1801 Effingham County Georgia Recorded in Book C, Page 95.

"Large Class Confirmed by Rev. P. Barry: Sacrament of Confirmation Administered to 115 Persons; One of Number over 100 Years Old." *Key West Citizen.* February 6, 1933, p. 7.

"Law's Technicality Frees a Murderer." *Tampa Tribune.* 15 Nov 1903, pg. 6

MacCauley, Clay (1843-1925). "The Seminole Indians of Florida", *Fifth Annual Report of the Bureau of Ethnology to the Secretary of the Smithsonian Institution*, 1883-'84, published by the United States Government Printing Office, Washington, D.C., Digital Collection. 1887, pages 469-531. https://www.flutopedia.com/refs/MacCauley_1887_TheSeminole IndiansOfFlorida_FP.pdf

Mahler, Carol. "Pine Level Townsite makes it to the National Register of Historic Places!" Originally published in the Arcadian, Oct 9, 2014; Section: Arcadian; Page: AS11. http://www.flpublicarchaeology.org/blog/wcrc/2014/10/13/pine -level-townsite-makes-it-to-the-national-register-of-historic-places/ Accessed Dec 31 2018

Alachua County, 1850. Joseph Meyer, Grosser Hand-Atlas uber alle Theile der Erde (Hillsburghaus, : Hildburghausen:

Bibliographischen Instituts, 1850) 148. Map Credit: Courtesy the private collection of Roy Winkelman. Description: Meyer's 1850 map of Florida is derived from the Tanner/Mitchell Universal atlas map of 1839, and similar to the 1845 maps. In this updated detail of Alachua County, waterways and townships are noted. http://fcit.usf.edu/florida/maps/pages/9900/f9931/f9931.htm

Map. Image Archives of the Historical Map & Chart Collection. Office of Coast Survey/National Ocean Service/NOAA. Sept 9 1861. https://historicalcharts.noaa.gov/

Map. Florida Office of the Surveyor General. A plat exhibiting the state of the surveys in the State of Florida with references., map, 1855; St. Augustine. (texashistory.unt.edu/ark:/67531/metapth220434/: accessed July 6, 2018), University of North Texas Libraries, The Portal to Texas History, texashistory.unt.edu; crediting University of Texas at Arlington Library.

Marchman, Watt P. Ed "The Ingraham. Everglades Exploring Expedition, 1892" *Tequesta: The Journal of the Historical Association of Southern Florida*, No. 7, 1947, *The Florida Historical Quarterly*, Vol. 26, No. 3 (Jan. 1948), pp. 264-274. http://www.jstor.org/stable/30139701

Marriage record of E. J. Hamilton and Rebecca Johnson. Ancestry.com. Florida, County Marriage Records, 1823-1982 [database on-line]. Lehi, UT, USA: Ancestry.com Operations, Inc., 2016. Original data: Marriage Records. Florida Marriages. Various Florida County Courthouses and State Archive, Tallahassee, Florida.

Meiklejohn, Don. "Some Moonshine Recipes." *The Palm Beach Post*, 27 Nov 1961, p. 4.

Monaco, C. S. 2012. "Alachua Settlers and the Second Seminole War." *The Florida Historical Quarterly*, Summer, 91 (1): 1–32. http://www.jstor.org/stable/23264821.

"More Pressure Tightens 'Lid' Upon Key West." *Miami News.* April 5, 1929.

"Monroe Sheriff, Believed Lost in Swamp, Returns." *Key West Citizen.* December 2, 1929.

"Monroe Sheriff Returns From Hunt for Fugitive." *Tampa Tribune.* December 2, 1929.

Moses, W.R., Record of the Everglade Exploration Expedition. https://ufdc.ufl.edu/AA00007669/00001

"Murderers are Riddled: Two Men Who Committed a Triple Murder are Shot to death by Posse of Florida Men." *Pensacola News Journal.* 27 Oct 1910, p. 1.

National Park Service. *Pioneer Settlement - Everglades National Park.* 2015.

National Park Service. *Historic Roads.* https://www.nps.gov/ever/learn/historyculture/historic-roads.htm. Last Updated April 14, 2015.

Native American Applications for Enrollment in Five Civilized Tribes (overturned), 1896. (Walter is listed on the roll as W.V. Hamilton.) Washington, D.C.: National Archives and Records Administration, n.d.

"Notice of Condemnation." Key West Citizen, December 2, 1950, p. 7.

"The notorious outlaw and negro desperado…" *Fort Myers Press.* June 29, 1899. Newspapers.com.

Novick, Peter. *That Noble Dream.* Cambridge: Cambridge University Press, 1988.

Oh, Intaek. *Peter Matthiessen and Ecological Imagination*

https://books.google.com/books?id=LqNiC5rCLIQC&pg=PA49
&lpg=PA49&dq=eugene+hamilton+chokoloskee&source=bl&ots
=DzKPhCGNBH&sig=Au9RYhpJleQgHNGaSPKsAQ2oEa0&hl
=en&sa=X&ved=2ahUKEwil49mgvNTcAhUjq1kKHfUKB1I4Ch
DoATAAegQIARAB#v=onepage&q=eugene%20hamilton%20ch
okoloskee&f=false

Obituary. Richard Hamilton. *Key West Citizen*. Thursday, February 3, 1944

Pensacola News Journal. "Murderers are Riddled: Two Men Who Committed a Triple Murder are Shot to death by Posse of Florida Men." 27 Oct 1910, page 1

Perdichizzi, Betsy. The Weeks Family: Southwest Florida Pioneers. 26 May 2005. http://www.zwire.com/site/news.cfm?BRD=2256&dept_id=4577 01&newsid=14588268&PAG=461&rfi=9

Probate Records. Florida, Manatee County, Vol G-H, 1872-1936, page 2122, Manatee, Florida. Property Records Ocala (Newnansville). 1 May 1855. CERTIFICATE No. 2540, page number 207?

Property Records Ocala (Newnansville). 25 Feb 1857. CERTIFICATE No. 2315, page number 70?

Property Tax Digests, Georgia, , 1793-1892: William P Edwards 1852 District 737 Taylor, Georgia. Source Citation Militia District Number: *737.* Source Information Ancestry.com. *Georgia, Property Tax Digests, 1793-1892* [database on-line]. Provo, UT, USA: Ancestry.com Operations, Inc., 2011. Original data: *Georgia Tax Digests [1890]. 140 volumes.* Morrow, Georgia: Georgia Archives.

"Refusal of Job by WPA Heads Irks Key West**Error! Bookmark not defined.** Centenarian." *Miami News.* Sun Feb 27 1938.

Richardson, Joe M. "Florida Black Codes." *The Florida Historical Quarterly* 47, no. 4 (1969): 365-79. http://www.jstor.org/stable/30140241.

"Robert E. Hamilton 101 years old seeks work on Relief Roll." *Key West**Error! Bookmark not defined.** Citizen*. December 15, 1933, p. 1.

Rogers, Bill. "Novel tarnishes woman's cherished memories." *Golden Gate Nugget*. August 9 1990.

Roussillon-Constanty, Laurence, Philippe Murillo, editors. *Science, Fables and Chimeras: Cultural Encounters*

https://books.google.com/books?id=A2ExBwAAQBAJ&pg=PA 245&lpg=PA245&dq=eugene+hamilton+chokoloskee&source=bl &ots=HIO3NSkL3y&sig=ZOxlF-kpDUv_4iJpnsGXNxgME6c&hl=en&sa=X&ved=2ahUKEwiF3fr YudTcAhUSw1kKHdNPClwQ6AEwDnoECAEQAQ#v=onepag e&q=eugene%20hamilton%20chokoloskee&f=false

"Saw a Million Florida Islands." *Tampa Tribune*, 28 Feb 1900. pg 6

Seabrook, William. Paradise U.S.A. *American Weekly*, 1944.

Seminole National Museum. "The Seminole Wars." *The Seminole Nation Museum*. *https://www.seminolenationmuseum.org/history/seminole-nation/the-seminole-wars/*

"Sheriff Niles of Monroe is Lost in Wilds." *Tampa Times*. November 30, 1929.

"Sheriff Niles of Monroe is Lost in Wilds." *Tampa Times*. November 30, 1929.

Shirley, Glenn. Belle Starr and Her Times: The Literature, the Facts, and the Legends. University of Oklahoma Press, 2015.

Short, Henry. The National Archives at Washington, D.C.; Washington, D.C.; Series Title: *U.S. Citizen Passenger Lists of Vessels Arriving at Key West, Florida*; NAI Number: *2790482*; Record Group Title: *Records of the Immigration and Naturalization Service, 1787 - 2004*; Record Group Number: *85*

Slave Schedules. 1850 U.S. Federal Census - Slave Schedules [database on-line]. Provo, UT, USA: Ancestry.com Operations Inc, 2004. Original data: United States of America, Bureau of the Census. Seventh Census of the United States, 1850. Washington, D.C.: National Archives and Records Administration, 1850. M432, 1,009 rolls.

Slave Schedules [database on-line]. 1860 U.S. Federal Census - Provo, UT, USA: Ancestry.com Operations Inc, 2010. Original data: United States of America, Bureau of the Census. Eighth Census of the United States, 1860. Washington, D.C.: National Archives and Records Administration, 1860. M653, 1,438 rolls.

Sleight, Frederick W. A Preview of Archaeology in the Ten Thousand Islands of Florida. *Kiva*, Vol. 7, No. 2 (Nov., 1941), pp. 5-8. Taylor & Francis, Ltd. on behalf of the Arizona Archaeological and Historical Society, Stable URL: http://www.jstor.org/stable/30246867

Smithsonian Institution. Miscellaneous Papers Relating to Anthropology, 1883. Original from Harvard University. Digitized Dec 5, 2007

Society for the Diffusion of Useful Knowledge (Great Britain), Murchison, I, Lubbock, John, Smith, Philip, Woodward, S.P, Key, T. Hewett, J. & C. Walker, *The Antilles or West India Islands,The Family Atlas Containing Eighty Maps, Constructed By Eminent Geographers, And Engraved On Steel, Under The Superintendence Of The Society For The Diffusion Of Useful Knowledge, Including The Geological Map Of England And Wales,* 1865. By Sir I. Murchison, F.R.S., The Star Maps By Sir John Lubbock, Bart. And The Plans Of London And Paris, With The New Discoveries And Other Improvements

To The Latest Date. And An Alphabetical Index. London: Edward
Stanford, 6, Charing Cross. 1865, Antilles or West India Islands.
Retrieved from the Digital Public Library of America, Digital
Collection.
https://www.davidrumsey.com/luna/servlet/detail/RUMSEY~8
~1~252480~5518495

Spessard Stone, edited by. From Storter, G. W. "Early Pioneers of
Collier County." *Naples News Tribune*, August 18, 1927

Stone, Spessard, editor. "Arcadia, Florida Early History." *The
Tampa Morning Tribune,* Tampa, Florida, January 10, 1909
http://freepages.rootsweb.com/~crackerbarrel/genealogy/Arcadia
1.html

Stout, Wesley. *"Barber's Razor Used On Throat In Florida Keys."*
Orlando Sentinel. Nov 9, 1965.

Summary Report. Case of Stephen Barrett, Orig. No. 996,404, and
Sarah Barrett, Orig. No. 531,374.

Szucs, Loretto Dennis, "Research in Census Records." In *The
Source: A Guidebook of American Genealogy,* ed. Loretto Dennis Szucs
and Sandra Hargreaves Luebking (Salt Lake City: Ancestry, 1997).

Tebeau, Charlton W. *Man in the Everglades*. University of Miami
Press, 1968

Thomas, Fred. "Ah ha! Sleuthing News Hound on Local Sailors
Trail" *Tampa Bay Times*. St. Petersburg, Pinellas, Florida, United
States of America. Sun, Aug 08, 1920 · Page 6

"Two Key Westers Picked up Drifting in Gulf Stream are Taken
into Cuba." *Key West Citizen*. 14 April 1930. Newspapers.com.

Truesdell, William G. *A Guide to the Wilderness Waterway - Everglades,
Florida*, p. 50.

U.S. Army Corps of Engineers."You Just Can't Live Without It": Ethnographic Study and Evaluation of Traditional Cultural Properties of the Modern Gladesmen Culture, Jacksonville, Florida, July 17, 2011 • Revised Draft

U.S., World War I Draft Registration Cards, 1917-1918 [database on-line]. Provo, UT, USA: Ancestry.com Operations Inc, 2005. (John Leon Hamilton. Registration State: *Florida*; Registration County: *Monroe*; Roll: *1556877*)

Verrill, A. Hyatt. Romantic And Historic Florida. https://archive.org/details/in.ernet.dli.2015.155824

"View of homes, Key West, Fla." *The Miriam and Ira D. Wallach Division of Art, Prints and Photographs: Photography Collection,* The New York Public Library. 1865.Digital Collection. Retrieved from http://digitalcollections.nypl.org/items/510d47e0-4e9d-a3d9-e040-e00a18064a99

Vignoles, Charles Blacker, and Henry Schenck Tanner. Map of Florida. [S.l, 1823] Map. https://www.loc.gov/item/2003627045/.

Ware, Lynn W. "The Peace River: A Forgotten Highway." *Tampa Bay History*, Vol 6 No 2, Fall/Winter 1984.

Warner, I. W. *The Immigrant's Guide and Citizen's Manual.* New York, 1848.

Watson, Ch. "History of the 10,000 Islands etc." 1927. Retrieved from The Copeland Papers, p. 1085. http://www.naplesnative.com/Documents/The%20Copeland%20Papers%20Part%201.pdf

Watson, G. H. Letter to unknown. Everglade, Florida, 1902

Watson, James G. "Man Writing: The Watson Trilogy: Peter Matthiessen in Archive." *Texas Studies in Literature and Language* 46, no. 2 (2004): 245-70. http://www.jstor.org/stable/40755411, Page 247

Webb, William. *"The Ancestry of Herbert Mitchell Webb and Inez Rosilie Edwards"*, 1985.

WEBBER, CARL. *EDEN OF THE SOUTH: Descriptive of the Orange Groves, Vegetable Farms, Strawberry Fields,... Peach Orchards, Soil, Climate, Natural Peculiariti. S.l.:* FORGOTTEN BOOKS, 2016.

'"White Lightning' Hit By High Living Cost." *Palm Beach Post.* Feb 21 1951. Newspaper.com.

Williams, W. Thorne. Sherman & Smith. Bonner's map of the State of Georgia with the addition of its geological features. Savannah [Ga.] 1849. Library of Congress Geography and Map Division Washington, D.C. 20540-4650 USA dcu. Digital Id

https://hdl.loc.gov/loc.gmd/g3921c.ct009970

Works Progress Administration, Historical Records Survey. State Library of Florida. *Brief history of DeSoto County, Florida* collected by the Works Progress Administration's Historical Records Survey., ca. 1939

Yelton, Susan. "Newnansville: A Lost Florida Settlement" The *Florida Historical Quarterly* Vol. 53, No. 3 (Jan., 1975), pp. 319-331 Published by: Florida Historical Society: http://www.jstor.org/stable/30145963 Page Count: 13

Young, Jeffrey R. "Slavery in Antebellum Georgia." New Georgia Encyclopedia. 26 July 2017. Web. 09 February 2019.

Images

Fig. 1.1 William Pitts Edwards (Ancestry.com)

Map 1.1 Springfield, Georgia year

Fig. 1.2 Effingham Living History Museum, Springfield Georgia (Photo: Karen Yvonne Hamilton)

Fig. 1.3 Effingham Living History Museum Main Building, Springfield Georgia (Photo: Karen Yvonne Hamilton)

Fig. 1.4 Land Records of Obadiah Edwards' property in Springfield, GA

Fig. 1.5 1826 GA Obadiah Edwards' property in Springfield, GA

Fig. 1.6 The only known image of Peggy Hamilton (Ancestry.com)

Fig. 1.7 Richard Hamilton's baptismal certificate

Fig. 1.8 The only photograph of Richard as a young man

Map 2.1 Alachua County, Florida

Fig. 2.1 Land for Sale Poster

Fig. 2.2 Land Records Newnansville, Florida, 1852

Fig. 2.3 Land Records Newnansville, Florida, 1852

Fig. 2.4 Believed to be Eleanor Edwards (Ancestry.com)

Fig. 2.5 Edwards' homestead in Williston, Florida, 2018. (Photo: Karen Yvonne Hamilton)

Figure 3.1 Barrett case folder cover

Map 4.1 Newly divided counties Manatee and Desoto Rand McNally 1892

Fig. 4.1. Author at the site of the Old Pine Level Courthouse, 2018 (Photo: Karen Yvonne Hamilton)

Fig. 4.2 We did manage to locate the infamous 'hanging tree' where it is rumored many a criminal swung. (Photo: Karen Yvonne Hamilton)

Fig. 5.1 George Christian (Ancestry.com)

Fig. 5.2 Sarah "Sally" Weeks (Ancestry.com, Iris Williams)

Map 6.1 Vignoles, Charles Blacker, and Henry Schenck Tanner. 1823

Fig. 7.1 Walter Joseph Valentine Hamilton

Fig. 7.2 Walter and Lettie Pent Hamilton. Lostmans River and Key West Florida.

Fig. 11.3 Buddy's three boys: William Joseph Hamilton, Jr. Francis Salvador Theodore Hamilton, and Ernest Eugene Hamilton, circa 1935

Fig. 11.4 Unidentified woman on one of the keys in the 10,000 Islands

Fig. 11.5 Remains of Gene Hamilton's cisterns on Wood Key

Fig. 11.6 Remains of Gene Hamilton's cisterns on Wood Key

Fig. 11.7 Ernest E. Hamilton, Jr. examining the remains of his great-grandfather's cistern on Wood Key.

Map 11.1 Hamilton Mound

Fig. 11.8 unidentified man & women fishing on beach

Fig. 11.9 Back of photo reads "Taken April 1 1928 Losman's River Fla."

Fig. 11.10 Floating Fish House (Ancestry.com, courtesy of Iris Williams)

Fig. 11.11 Floating Fish House (Ancestry.com, courtesy of Iris Williams)

Fig. 11.12 Unidentified men with alligator

Fig. 11.13 Rosalie and Nellie Hamilton. Both married into the Gomes family.

Fig. 11.14 Rebecca Johnson Hamilton with the children

Fig. 12.1 Rebecca Hamilton, King Gene Hamilton and Butterball Knowles. Photographed for an article written by William Seabrook in 1944

Fig. 12.2 William David Parker (Ancestry.com. Iris Williams)

Fig. 13.1. Advertisement for Poinciana. Romance and Riches Still Lurk in the Curves of Lostman's River. The Miami News. 23 Oct 1925.

Fig. 13.2 Advertisement for Poinciana. Fisher Folk. The Miami News. 3 Jan 1926.

Fig. 13.3 Advertisement for Poinciana. The Giant Avocados. The Tampa Tribune. 23 Feb 1926.

Fig. 13.4 Joaquin 'King' Gomes (Ancestry.com)

Fig. 13.5 Advertisement King used for his charter business (Newspapers.com)

Fig. 13.6 Joseph 'Josie' Hamilton (Ancestry.com, courtesy of Iris Williams)

Map 14.1 Shark Point and Graveyard Creek, 2019 (Google Maps)

Fig. 14.1 William 'Buddy' Hamilton

Fig. 14.2 Robert Hamilton There has some debate from family members as to whether the photo of Robert shown here is indeed Robert Hamilton or his brother, Henry.

Fig. 14.3 Authorities brought a teacher down to Lostmans but Buddy knew more than the teacher, so they fired the teacher and Buddy taught the class. He is on the far left of this photo. (Paul Gomes)

Fig. 14.4 Salvador Gomes on the left, William Joseph Hamilton on the right, seated is Eugene Joseph Hamilton King Gene). King Gene was a lawman for a while in the islands.

Fig. 14.5 William 'Buddy' Hamilton on Lostmans River, circa 1927

Fig. 14.6 Ellen and William 'Buddy' Hamilton

Fig. 14.7 William 'Buddy' Hamilton

Fig. 14.8 Florinda Gomes Hamilton and William 'Bill' Parker

Fig. 14.9 Florinda Gomes Hamilton Parker with her and Buddy's sons. Top: Francis Salvador Theodore, Ernest Eugene. Bottom: Flo and William Joseph, Jr. (Junior)

Fig. 15.1 Richard Hamilton 101 years old

About the Author

Karen Yvonne Hamilton grew up hearing stories from her father and uncles about their lives growing up on Lostmans River. Those stories instilled in her a great passion for the islands and an intense desire to learn more about her family history and South Florida.

Hamilton lives in Southeast Florida and is a former English teacher. She has spent the past 30 years researching her family history and life in the Everglades. Her educational background includes a BA in English and coursework towards an MFA in Creative Writing. Hamilton has published essays with Heritage Press, Florida Living magazine, and the St. Pauls Review, and was a finalist in the 2017 New Letters Award in Creative Nonfiction.

Lifetales Media
Hamilton's organization, *Lifetales Media*, offers assistance in recording lifestories and organizing those stories into print, providing descendants with a lasting memory for their families. In

addition, Hamilton offers memoir writing workshops and editing and layout help for those wishing to publish their lifestories.

Her motto is "Preserving history...one lifestory at a time."

.

Made in the USA
Coppell, TX
25 June 2021